Saving Afghanistan

First published in 2009
by

ACADEMIC FOUNDATION
4772-73 / 23 Bharat Ram Road, (23 Ansari Road),
Darya Ganj, New Delhi - 110 002 (India).
Phones : 23245001 / 02 / 03 / 04.
Fax : +91-11-23245005.
E-mail : academic@vsnl.com
www. academicfoundation.com

in association with :

Institute for Defence Studies and Analyses, New Delhi
www.idsa.in

Cataloging in Publication Data--DK
Courtesy: D.K. Agencies (P) Ltd. <docinfo@dkagencies.com>

Asian Security Conference (10th : 2008 : New Delhi, India)
Saving Afghanistan / editors, V. Krishnappa, Shanthie Mariet D'Souza and Priyanka Singh.
p. Cm.
Papers presented at the 10th Asian Security Conference,
held at New Delhi on 4th February 2008.
Includes index.
ISBN 13: 9788171887538
ISBN 10: 8171887538

1. Afghanistan--Politics and government--2001- --Congresses. 2. Conflict management--Afghanistan--Congresses. 3. Afghanistan--Strategic aspects--Congresses. 4. Nation-building--Afghanistan--Congresses. 5. Postwar reconstruction--Afghanistan--Congresses. I. Krishnappa, V. II. Shanthie Mariet D'Souza III. Singh, Priyanka, 1980- IV. Title.

DDC 320.9581 22

Typeset by Italics India, New Delhi.
Printed and bound in India.

Contents

About the Editors/Contributors

Editors:

V. Krishnappa is a Research Fellow at the Institute for Defence Studies and Analysis (IDSA) New Delhi. His research interests include strategic dynamics in South and West Asia, great power politics, strategic theory, transnational terrorism and contemporary wars. He is the Book Review Editor of the *Strategic Analysis* (IDSA-Routledge) and Member of Editorial Committee of *Journal of Defence Studies* (IDSA)

Shanthie Mariet D'Souza is Associate Fellow at the IDSA, New Delhi. Her research interests and expertise includes United States policy towards Afghanistan, terrorism and strategies in counter-terrorism, non-state armed groups and armed conflicts in South Asia, global war on terrorism, Afghan insurgency and the counter-insurgency campaign.

Priyanka Singh is a Research Assistant in the IDSA, New Delhi. She holds an Honours degree in Political Science from Lady Shri Ram College, University of Delhi and a PhD in Indo-US Relations from the University of Lucknow.

Contributors:

A.K. Antony is Minister of Defence, Government of India (GoI), New Delhi.

Indranil Banerjie is the Founder and Executive Director of the SAPRA India Foundation, New Delhi.

Anup Kumar Datta is Professor, Department of Political Science, University of North Bengal, Darjeeling.

C. Christine Fair is a senior political scientist with the RAND Corporation, Washington D.C.

Ali A. Jalali is currently Distinguished Professor at the Near East South Asia Center for Strategic Studies (NESA), Washington D.C. and a researcher at the Institute for National Strategic Studies (INSS), Washington D.C.

Seth G. Jones is Adjunct Professor at Edmund A. Walsh School of Foreign Service, Georgetown University and a Political Scientist at the RAND Corporation, Washington D.C.

Rasul Bakhsh Rais is Professor of Political Science and Head, Department of Social Sciences, Lahore University of Management Sciences (LUMS).

Anita Inder Singh is currently Visiting Professor at the Centre for Peace and Conflict Resolution, Jamia Millia Islamia, New Delhi.

Seema Sridhar is a doctoral candidate at the School of International Studies, Jawaharlal Nehru University (JNU).

Introduction

This book is about the future of Afghanistan which seems to be rapidly slipping into chaos. It contains perspectives of experts on counter-insurgency and nation-building in Afghanistan who debated the issues in a conference at the Institute for Defence Studies and Analyses (IDSA) in February 2008. Although the Conference discussed a range of themes important to Asian security, the chapters in this volume focus on some key issues like, the character of the conflict in Afghanistan; the role of regional actors; the nature of engagement of the US and its allies; the assessment of the future course of action by major actors and the role played by INGOs and the international community at large. More significantly, the experts sought to answer the crucial question: what can be done to stabilise Afghanistan? This volume is a collection of their insightful papers.

In his chapter "Afghanistan: Struggle to Regain Momentum", Ali A. Jalali, distinguished Afghan scholar and diplomat, asserts that Afghanistan faces the distinct possibility of sliding back into instability and chaos. Afghanistan is challenged by a revitalised Taliban-led insurgency, record rise in drug production, erosion of the rule of law and a weakening national government in the regions outside the major cities. All of this is happening just at a time when the situation in Pakistan and the strategic context around Afghanistan is in a state of flux. Jalali identifies key drivers of instability in Afghanistan and argues that to achieve stability it is necessary to focus on three inter-related aspects of the Afghan problem: governance, drugs and the insurgency.

In her chapter "Reconstructing Afghanistan", Anita Inder Singh traces the origins of America's Global War on Terror in Afghanistan, where the Taliban government harboured Osama bin Laden. The author addresses key questions that are axiomatic to the ongoing debate: What are the linkages between NATO's aims in Afghanistan and American global strategy? What are the key challenges before the coalition? What is their strategy and how well is it working? What needs to be done to enhance legitimacy and build stable institutions in Afghanistan? And what is the role of international intervention in shaping the future of Afghanistan? After a survey of important developments in the post-Taliban period, the author offers some useful suggestions for nation-building in post-Taliban Afghanistan.

Seth G. Jones in "Afghanistan Redux" asks two interrelated questions: First, why do insurgencies begin in general? Second, what are the origins of the Afghanistan insurgency? Drawing on his considerable knowledge as a RAND expert on insurgency and terrorism, Jones discusses the historical evolution of counter-insurgency doctrines and in that light, examines the rise of insurgency in Afghanistan. Jones concludes that the Afghan insurgency "will ultimately be won or lost in the rural areas of Afghanistan, not in the cities." Therefore, "providing security to the villages, especially in strategically important areas of the South and East" will be the key to success in Afghanistan.

In his chapter "The Future of Afghanistan: Appraising Alternatives", Rasul Bakhsh Rais, an eminent Pakistani expert and observer of the Afghanistan scene, takes stock of the current turmoil in a historical and geographical framework. He constructs his narrative around two propositions: First, Afghanistan's process of establishing a modern state started late, with a meagre institutional endowment and a convenient "rentier" mindset. Two, the "frontier" character of the state constrained what the Afghan nation-builders aspired for, and narrowed the scope of what realistically could be achieved. Following an insightful survey of the recent developments, he concludes that 'in terms of history, terrain, legacy and the nature of the task, Afghanistan poses one of the greatest challenges in post-conflict reconstruction.' Failure of nation and state-building, he contends, will have disastrous consequences for the entire international community. This is one of those collaborative international efforts whose success will make every country a victor and its failure every one a loser. He calls upon Afghan leaders and their neighbours to bring to bear greater responsibility and show greater wisdom in their engagement in the post-conflict reconstruction.

Pakistani attitude towards militancy in the region is discussed by C. Christine Fair in her chapter. She addresses the key policy puzzle: how the international community and indeed anti-militant elements within the Pakistani government can support the large majorities of Pakistanis who feel threatened by the various militant groups while at the same time, mobilising them to embrace the war on terrorism as a conflict for Pakistan's own survival as a modern and moderate Muslim state. Resolution of this puzzle is not only important to the future of Pakistan, but for the entire region. Fair's survey offers some useful insights that the policy-makers in the region can benefit from. Besides, the author offers the readers rich data that could be a useful starting point for further research on this important question.

In her chapter "Taking Stock of the Afghan Conflict: External-Internal Dimensions", Shanthie Mariet D'Souza, provides an overview of external-internal dimensions of the Afghan conflict. She begins by asserting that the international forces are floundering because they fail to understand the nature and complexity of insurgency in Afghanistan. In addition, America's unwillingness to apply sufficient resources to counter-insurgency has created a permissive environment for the Taliban to reassert in ways unanticipated by the American and NATO partners. She identifies ungoverned spaces, compromised security, inadequate economic assistance and conflicting agendas of NATO partners as critical areas that need special international efforts to succeed.

Anup Datta asserts that the existence of rival power centres and diffusion of arms among the well resourced militias competing for power and influence, are posing a serious challenge to nation-building and post-conflict reconstruction efforts. In the chapter titled, "Post-Taliban Afghanistan: Conflict, Violence and Regional

Stability", he argues that the absence of coherent central authority and unified effort among varied actors has undermined rebuilding efforts. The al-Qaeda and its remnants are still active in the southern and eastern parts of the country and are at large on both sides of the Pakistan-Afghanistan border as well as the militant Islamic cadres who create irritants in the Jammu & Kashmir border. Datta warns that India's interests in Central Asia would be at stake if Taliban resurgence is not halted.

In his chapter "The Problem of Institution Building in Afghanistan", Indranil Banerjie, provides an overview of the origins of the Afghan conflict and discusses the traditional basis of power-sharing and recent attempts at democratisation. He emphasises the importance of institution-building as a key to rebuilding trust and deepening of democratic processes. Banerjie identifies lack of political will and ethnic divide as key obstacles to institution-building. He warns that without viable political institutions the space will be occupied by more traditional actors and armed groups, thus endangering the process of democratisation in Afghanistan.

In her chapter "Civil-Military Engagement in Post-Conflict Reconstruction: A Study of Provincial Reconstruction Teams", Seema Sridhar examines and analyses the contribution of the PRTs to the security situation in Afghanistan. The chapter locates ongoing peace operations and the evolution of PRTs in their historical context. The author finds that the presence of numerous actors and incoherent control structures has undermined the utility of PRTs.

This book offers readers with rich perspectives on the ongoing developments within Afghanistan and its neighbourhood. The contributors bring to the debate unique insights from their vantage points. The book would be a useful read for students, scholars and diplomats interested in Afghanistan and the region.

Our grateful thanks are due to the contributors for their generosity, cooperation and patience in making this year-long effort bear fruit. We would also like to thank a large number of our colleagues at the Institute without whose willing help and support this task could not have been completed in time. We also owe special thanks to Dr. Thomas Mathew, Dr. M. Mayilvaganan, Ms. Medha Bisht, Dr. Pankaj Jha, Ms. Priyadarshini Singh, Vivek Kaushik and Ms. Ameeta Narang for their help in the organisation of the Tenth Asian Security Conference.

V. Krishnappa
Shanthie Mariet D'Souza
Priyanka Singh

1

Globalisation, Non-State Armed Groups and the Changing Nature of Conflicts

A.K. ANTONY

Of late, the Asian region has acquired a unique centrality in global strategic affairs. The challenges for the Asian region—and indeed all the nations the world over are of a similar nature. Terrorism, nuclear proliferation, and sectarian conflicts are some of the issues that require our urgent and focused attention.

Today, the world has truly become a global village. Thus, security of nations cannot be restricted to narrow geographical and political boundaries.

With increasing globalisation, it is often argued that the chances of the breakout of a conventional war are remote. All the same, we have to be eternally vigilant and ever-prepared for any eventuality.

In recent years, conflicts have broken out between states and non-state players. Such conflicts are differently categorised as civil war, insurgency, ethnic conflict, irregular war, or even terrorism. The nature of conflicts notwithstanding, it is the civilian population that bears the brunt of such conflicts. The traditional distinction between soldiers and the civilians is increasingly being obliterated, for both are targets for terrorists.

It is well-known that no price is too high for the security of a nation. Global defence expenditure during the 1990s had registered a marginal decline. However, of late, global defence expenditure has registered a sharp upward growth.

The world today realises that no nation can consider itself to be immune from terrorism. The lessons learnt elsewhere can prove to be useful in devising our policies. Similarly, other nations too can benefit from our experiences. Nations must devise ways and means to cooperate to effectively counter terrorism.

Increasing use of information technology will mean that wars in future will be hi-tech, intense, yet brief. The mobility and destructive capacity of weapons has gone up several times. Experts apprehend that with proliferation of technologies—particularly information technology, space technology, biotechnology, nanotechnology and genetic engineering will only multiply the lethal force of new weapons.

Nuclear proliferation continues to be a serious challenge for mankind. I am sure that experts attending this Conference will deliberate on the future of the nuclear order, its relevance and implications for security of the Asian region.

The emergence of non-state players is another grave challenge confronting all nations. These non-state players do not recognise any territorial boundaries. They utilise latest global communication and transport networks and rely on garnering international support. Their common objective is to disturb existing state apparatus, destabilise neighbouring states and create new states based on ethno-cultural identity. Most of these non-state players are not fighting for a national identity or territory and have abstract notions of carving out a separate and unique identity of their own based on ethnicity, religious and tribal basis. According to estimates of Military Balance, out of the 343 non-state armed groups operating in the world, 187 groups operate in the Asian region.

India has been the target of disruptive elements for several years. Major powers of the world then believed that they would be immune to such elements and had, as such, little sympathy for our concerns. However, now all nations realise and accept the need for greater cooperation in effectively meeting such challenges.

Another important issue that has a direct bearing on Asian security in the Twenty-first century is the generic issue of fragile states and nation building, as demonstrated by the increasing instability in Afghanistan. Trends indicate that international efforts at nation building are faltering on many counts. This is a potentially dangerous situation.

The principal challenges that Asia and other regions of the world are likely to face are transnational, or have the potential of becoming transnational. While we must be guard against the outbreak of conventional wars, we must recognise that newer forms of conflict are more likely. The following measures can help the Asian states in meeting various challenges effectively.

The first one is to maintain an active dialogue process, not only among governments, but also defence establishments to build strong channels of communication and dispel mistrust.

Secondly, we must develop mechanisms to share intelligence about terror groups, criminal elements, drug cartels and other transnational networks that foment violence and subvert states.

Thirdly, we must attempt to devise common solutions to common challenges that threaten our collective security. We need to develop multilateral frameworks to promote dialogue and prepare strategies for cooperative action.

2

Afghanistan: The Struggle to Regain Momentum

ALI A. JALALI

Seven years into the US-led military invasion, the crisis in Afghanistan is worsening. The country is challenged by a revitalised Taliban-led insurgency, a record rise in drug production, deterioration in the rule of law, and a weakening of the national government's influence in the regions outside of the major cities. Whatever good news there is, is overshadowed by the bad news.

Following the ouster of the Taliban in 2001, Afghanistan scored numerous achievements in its transition to democracy; notably in rebuilding its state institutions. Afghanistan adopted a modern constitution, held peaceful presidential and parliamentary elections, created national security institutions, improved women's rights, and expanded education. The Afghans are freer today. But while this progress is notable, the current troubles come as a result of what was not done in the last seven years.

Afghanistan was the least resourced of any American-led nation-building operation. There are 1.5 international soldiers for every 1000 persons in Afghanistan compared to 20.5 per 1000 in Kosovo, 19 in Bosnia, 10 in Sierra Leone, and nearly 4 in Haiti.[1] Post-conflict stabilisation operations require more troops and longer time than to win the initial fight. In fighting, firepower and technology enable smaller, more agile forces to prevail. But in post-conflict stabilisation and reconstruction, there is a need for more ground troops, money, and time. Low levels of investment in military power and economic assistance in post-conflict reconstruction lead to low levels of security, ineffective governance, and poor economic growth.

1. UNDP (2007). *Afghanistan Human Development Report 2007*. p.54

The key to stabilisation is curbing the ability and desire of former combatants to renew the violence, while creating a national capacity to transform the war-ravaged structures into peace-building institutions. It is a multifaceted procedure of "breaking" and "making". Breaking down the war machines is a prerequisite for creating the institutions that will be capable of sustaining peace. Failure in this can lead to renewal of fighting and proliferation of criminal activity and banditry. Deactivating the war machines is an immediate need; making them useless is a long-term goal. The war machines must be made obsolete and their use made irrelevant—there should be no space for recruitment into warring militias and no support for actors who want to continue the cycle of violence.

From the outset, two contradictory concepts drove international intervention in Afghanistan. The country was described as the major front of a global war on terror, yet the intervention was a "light footprint" engagement. This "light footprint" continues to impair every aspect of reconstruction in Afghanistan. The Taliban were removed from power, but neither their potential to return nor their external support was addressed. Co-opting criminal networks for tactical gains left many of the traditional combatants in place and perpetuated the influence of the most notorious human rights violators. The focus on accomplishing short-term security goals undermined the efforts at establishing positive long-term trends. Failure to adopt a comprehensive and integrated approach to combating narcotics led to record increases in illicit drug production, which fuels corruption and funds terrorism and criminality. Inefficient use of insufficient funds, which is mostly outside of Afghan government control, failed to create economic opportunities, good governance, and rule of law.

Afghanistan faces the distinct threat of sliding back into instability and chaos. The troubles come amidst a changing political and military environment in and around Afghanistan that compounds any effective response to emerging challenges. Domestically, the political consensus of 2001 is being lost to disruptive factionalism. Re-assertive strongmen and political opportunists linked to criminal networks are forcing the weak government into political compromises and tactical deals. The regional actors who once collectively supported the post-

Taliban political transition now hold diverging views. Political changes in the region have strongly influenced the attitude of regional actors. Internationally, the coalition is divided. Nor have the coalition member-states come with the same level of political and military commitment.

There is, however, still hope that the decline can be reversed through a new strategic approach. The significant institutional, social, and economic achievements made during the past seven years provide a solid foundation for building a modern democratic state in Afghanistan. In public opinion polls Afghans consistently associate democracy with personal freedoms, equality and justice, and overwhelmingly support it. They do not see the Taliban or other non-state power holders as alternatives to the current political system.

This chapter examines the drivers of instability in Afghanistan and recommends ways to achieve stabilitv through institutional, conceptual and procedural change, focusing on three interrelated aspects of the Afghan problem: governance, drugs, and the insurgency.

Governance

Both state-building and governance in Afghanistan are troubled by diverging concepts that influence the policies of domestic, regional, and global actors on the scene. The numerous domestic and international actors come with an uneven level of commitment, different degrees of resources, procedures, and priorities. They are further hindered by a continued cycle of political and economic violence. In such an environment, competing demands for responding to these challenges are often hard to reconcile.

Good governance is hampered by a lack of state control over institutions and procedures. The basic functions of governance are performed by an array of state and non-state actors including foreign militaries, international bodies, non-governmental organisations, and informal/traditional domestic power holders. The state has even deferred the "monopoly of legitimate use of force" to foreign actors in the face of an unstable security situation, in the hope that it can manage to rebuild the state under the security cover of foreign militaries. While such a pattern is not uncommon in post-conflict and developing states, the slow pace of state building in Afghanistan has inhibited efficiency in governance, security, and economic development. Consequently, without the state controlling a central role, public goods contributed by different actors tend to be uncoordinated, unstable, transient, and more supply-driven than demand-driven.[2]

Afghanistan has made major strides in its transition to democracy. The government's legitimacy has been supported by the political participation of all the domestic stakeholders in adopting the constitution, and holding fair presidential and legislative elections. Yet the government's inability to establish the rule of law has frustrated these democratic achievements. The obsession over elections without sufficient investment in reconstruction undermined the legitimacy of the elections. The relatively early elections favoured warlords and militia leaders who influenced the polls with their money and guns. This significantly hindered long-term democratic goals. The fast-paced political process in Afghanistan was influenced mostly by the priorities of the international community and not the ground realities in the country. As the International Crisis Group noted, "The desire for a quick, cheap war followed by a quick, cheap peace is what has brought Afghanistan to the present, increasingly dangerous situation."[3]

The structural legitimacy of the current government suffers from a lack of capacity, particularly at the sub-national level, where the vacuum is filled by insurgents, militia commanders, and local criminal gangs, all of whom undermine human security, local governance, democratic values, and the delivery of basic services.[4] The shortfall is what Max Weber labelled as a lack of "rational-legal authority", which is obtainable only when rules, supported by institutions to enforce them, underpin popular acceptance of government.[5] The rapidly

2. See Nixon, Hamish (2007). *International Assistance and Governance in Afghanistan*, Heinrich Boell Foundation Publication Series on Promoting Democracy under Conditions of State Fragility, Volume 2. Berlin. June. pp.12–14.
3. International Crisis Group (2006). *Countering Afghanistan's Insurgency: No Quick Fixes*. Asia Report No. 123, 2 November.
4. See Afghanistan NGO Safety Office (ANSO) Report, *ANSO Quarterly DATA Report Dec 22, 2006–June 30, 2007*. The report states that the impunity of local power-brokers (predominantly former combatants but also religious and ethnic leaders) will continue to combine with limited law enforcement capacity to create an environment in which NGOs will continue to suffer criminally related fatalities going into 2008.
5. Weber, Max (1947). *The Theory of Social and Economic Organization*. New York: Oxford University Press. pp.130–2. Cited in Bill, James and Robert Springborg (1990). *Politics in the Middle East*. HarperCollins. p.38.

expanding insurgency in Afghanistan only amplifies a cascading process by providing an opportune environment for crime.[6] All of these factors, coupled with the insurgency-related violence in the south and south-east, and the inability of security forces to counter local criminals and drug lords, has led to a tremendous loss of public confidence.[7]

Although a series of new state-building projects opted for a "top-down" approach, the real political and military influence in the country remained a "bottom-up" trend. Strong efforts were made to enhance the capacity of the Central government and extend its influence into the provinces, from the top-down, but international security forces tackled the problem of violence by appealing to actors at the ground level, in a bottom-up approach. As the political process continued, the failure to build the institutional power of the Central government perpetuated the influence of regional factions. This situation could once again result in fragmentation of power, similar to the political scene during the civil war. As the United Nations Secretary-General recently informed the Security Council, security, institution-building, and development gains made since the 2001 ouster of the Taliban might "stall or even be reversed."[8]

Building effective governance at the provincial and district levels is the key to legitimacy and stabilisation. Currently, sub-national institutions mandated by the constitution are only partially established. While Community Development Councils have been created in some areas, allowing local leaders to have a direct influence over reconstruction projects, the introduction of other district, village, and municipal governance councils has been delayed indefinitely. Elected provincial councils are in place but are fraught with confusion regarding their role and responsibility. The resulting institutional vacuum inhibits the democratic process. The situation further complicates the coordination of sustained services to the local populace. Even the security-driven projects run by Provincial

---

6. See ANSO Report, n.4.
7. See, for example, Ibrahimi, Sayed Yaqub (2007). *Northern Afghanistan: The Enemy Within.* Institute for War and Peace Reporting (IWPR), 18 September.
8. AFP (2007). "UN Chief Calls for New Afghan Strategy against Insurgents", 26 September.

Reconstruction Teams (PRT)[9] and other groups sometimes conflict with the objectives of government institutions and processes, undermining their effectiveness.[10]

The key constraints to strengthening sub-national systems in Afghanistan are, first and foremost, the absence of a clear policy framework regarding a desired institutional structure and a strategy to implement it.[11] National ministries tend to be over-centralised, with offices in Kabul retaining functions that could be performed much more efficiently at lower levels of government. Provincial departments of central ministries are politically, financially and administratively linked directly to Kabul. The resulting stove-piping leaves little space for the local levels of government to function. Removal of existing perceptional and managerial divides between Kabul and the outlying regions is essential for defragmenting the current administrative process.

The rule of law is at the heart of any government's legitimacy and is a prerequisite for human security. In Afghanistan the international community has failed to place a high priority on reforming the law enforcement and justice sectors, with severe consequences. Excessive emphasis on security at the expense of the rule of law subordinates justice to security considerations and turns the police into a force primarily used for combating insurgents instead of protecting the populace and supporting law and order. Obviously, in conflict-ridden conditions there is a need to meet security threats head-on, and certainly the police forces often find themselves on the front lines of insurgent attacks. However, such an approach cannot make compromises in the administration of justice. It is, after all, the rule of law that contributes directly to the security of the nation and its people.

9. There are currently 25 PRTs led by 13 countries: 12 by USA (Farah, Qalat, Ghazni, Sharana, Khost, Gardez, Parwan, Mehtar-e Lam, Jalalabad, Assadabad, Nuristan, Panjsher); 2 by Germany (Faizabad and Kundoz); and 1 each by New Zealand (Bamian), Lithuania (Cheghcheran), Italy (Heart), Canada (Kandahar), the UK (Lashkargah), Norway (Maymana), Sweden (Mazar-e Sharif), Hungary (Pul-e Khomri), Spain (Qala-e Naw), the Netherlands (Tirin Kot), and Turkey (Maydan).

10. World Bank (2007). *Report on Service Delivery and Governance at the Sub-national Level in Afghanistan*. July.

11. World Bank (2007). *Report on Strengthening the Role of Government at Provincial, District and Community Levels Vital to Delivering Services*. July. pp.6–10.

The decline of the security situation in Afghanistan is often attributed to a lack of capacity required to respond to threats from domestic and external sources. Officials and observers cite the slow development of the Afghan security forces (army and police), poor infrastructure, and inadequate numbers of the US and NATO forces as reasons for the violence and instability. While all this is relevant, a much greater factor is the absence of strong and unified leadership. This absence combined with the lack of a shared vision capable of directing the efforts of the various actors is a formula for failure.

Finally, fighting corruption is a major challenge. According to the annual survey (2007) by Transparency International, Afghanistan ranks 172 out of 180 countries in the *Corruption Perceptions Index.*[12] The human, financial, and time-related costs of corruption are very high. It erodes public confidence in government and deters private investment. The government's efforts to fight corruption are fragmented, selective, tactical, and reactive. Although solutions to the problem hinge on positive changes in security, economic development and the rule of law, there is a need for strategic action integrating prevention, detection, prosecution and sanction measures. Rising public awareness as well as behaviour and perceptual change are also essential.

The Drug Problem

Three major hurdles hamper any counter-narcotics campaign in Afghanistan. They include a record production of opium owing to the loss of state control, consolidation of the drug trade into a network of politicians and traffickers, and disagreement over any counter-narcotics strategy among representatives of the international community.

With a 34 per cent increase this year, opium production has peaked to 8200 metric tonnes.[13] A new geographic trend indicates that opium cultivation is no longer associated with poverty, but is more closely linked to greed and the insurgency. The major difference in this year's

12. Transparency International (2007). *Transparency International Corruption Perception Index.* p.4.
13. United Nations Office of Drugs and Crime (UNODC) (2007). "Executive Summary", *Afghanistan Opium Survey 2007*. pp.1–5.

poppy cultivation has been the growing divide between the north and the south, with significant poppy reductions in northern provinces and substantial increases in the south. Seventy per cent of the opium was produced in five troubled southern provinces where insurgency has intensified, giving credence to the belief that counter-insurgency missions are also counter-narcotics efforts. At the same time, defeating the insurgency in the south might reduce drug production in the area, but it will not solve the problem unless it is coupled with targeting the traffickers and helping farmers through a carefully crafted transitional strategy.

Consolidation of the drug economy into an organised network has created a parallel system that provides economic, financial, security, conflict resolution, and marketing services to the people. The network is organised into a chain of actors, facilitators, protectors, and political patrons. This includes poppy farmers, wage labourers, small opium traders, wholesalers and refiners, traffickers, local militia commanders, government officials, and political patrons. The network functions more effectively than the government. Leveraging poverty, lack of security and the rule of law in the country, it influences every aspect of political, social and economic life. Such a criminal economy significantly contributes to official corruption, insecurity, and the breakdown of the rule of law.

The Afghanistan *National Drug Control Strategy* aims to achieve a sustainable decrease in the cultivation, production, trafficking, and consumption of illicit drugs with a goal of complete elimination. Its four priorities are disrupting the trafficking network, providing alternative livelihood for farmers, reducing demand, and building institutions.[14] The strategy is endorsed by contributing nations, but there is chronic disagreement among some international partners over who to target first: traffickers or farmers. The United States favours spraying poppy fields with pesticides from the air, but the Afghan government has concerns that spraying might estrange poor farmers and drive them into the arms of the Taliban. The United Nations and NATO oppose spraying, with NATO refusing to get involved in

14. Department of the Army Headquarters (2006). "Counterinsurgency," FM3-24, December, p.1, at <*http//www.fas.org/irp/doddir/army/fm3-24.pdf*>

fighting traffickers or destroying drug labs and markets. Meanwhile, the lack of a decisive campaign against the traffickers has permitted them to consolidate their trade into networks with significant political backing—a possible prelude to a narco-state. Efforts to disrupt drug networks are stymied by the absence of any political will, the protection of traffickers by government officials, poor investigative capacity, and corruption in the police and judicial system.

Given the multidimensional nature of opium production in Afghanistan, counter-narcotics efforts should be integrated into every aspect of development: security, economic growth, and governance. There are no quick or simple solutions. Attempts to simplify the problem in order to make it more manageable and compatible with the domestic policies of donor countries rarely lead to sustained progress.

Fighting the Insurgency

The Taliban-led insurgency in Afghanistan is waged in a highly volatile socio-political environment. What drives people to fight is not merely the ideology, but rather the unstable environment and the influence of existing networks of tribes, clans, criminal networks, and transnational organisations. There are many independent but interlinked actors challenging the Afghan government and its international allies for various reasons. It is quite different from the insurgency of the 1980s, when a multi-factional Afghan resistance against the Soviet occupation was operationally fragmented, yet all groups determinedly fought for a common cause.

The new insurgents are an assortment of ideologically motivated Afghan and foreign militants, disillusioned tribal communities, foreign intelligence operatives, drug traffickers, militia commanders, disenchanted and unemployed youth, and self-interested spoilers. The insurgency is more of a political alliance of convenience than an ideological movement, and the various actors often have little coordination or strategic vision. The challenge in dealing with this insurgency is to separate the insurgents from the terrorist-minded militants. This can be achieved only by an integrated strategy of military and civilian operations.

The most serious problem in fighting insurgency is the absence of a coordinated strategy based on a shared vision and carried out through an integrated military, political, and developmental effort. The US military defines counter-insurgency as "military, paramilitary, political, economic, psychological and civic actions taken by a government to defeat insurgency." In Afghanistan there is little connection between tactical and strategic operations, between short-term and long-term goals. Nor are military and non-military operations coordinated and directed toward a common goal. Meanwhile, actions carried out by different partners, including NATO, the US-led Operation Enduring Freedom, the Afghan government, regional partners (Pakistan in particular), and others, are strategically fragmented.

NATO forces have won many battles against the insurgents in the South since 2006, but have seen little improvement in the strategic situation. Failure to consolidate military gains by holding and rebuilding areas cleared from insurgents has blocked any strategic improvement. Afghan security forces and allied contingents do not have sufficient forces to hold the ground, facilitate governance, and protect the people.[15] This situation hinders efforts to isolate the population from the insurgents, and win the hearts and minds of the people.[16]

Because of an insufficient number of troops on the ground, military commanders tend to use firepower as a force multiplier. Using long-range artillery and air strikes against insurgents hidden amongst the civilian population is not an ideal way to defeat the enemy. The resulting collateral damage and civilian casualties contribute to insecurity and popular resentment exploited by the Taliban. Recently, there have been demands for additional 7500 troops to augment the 42,000 NATO troops in Afghanistan. As of January 2008, the United States has announced sending 3200 marines to help foiling the Taliban's expected spring offensive. But the increase will have no major strategic impact unless other elements of the counter-insurgency operations are carried out in a coordinated way. Additional troops and

15. Ames, Paul (2007). "Challenges Mount in Afghanistan", Associated Press, 4 September.
16. BBC News (2007). "UK's Afghan Gains May be Lost", 28 September.

firepower will not help without good governance, sustainable security, and the establishment of the rule of law. In Musa Qalah, an area that was recently cleared of the Taliban, what one resident said reflects the prevailing opinion: that the people need security more than they want schools and roads.[17]

There is also little connection between the military and non-military counter-insurgency efforts carried out by different partners. NATO military action typically targets terrorists and insurgents in order to dissuade, deter and defeat them through combat action. But there is no clear owner either for the non-military part of the effort or for the overall strategy and campaign plan. Actions aimed at assuring, persuading and influencing the people, through the provision of human security, humanitarian assistance, basic services, infrastructure, institution building, and support for the rule of law are fragmented. It is a "free for all" sphere of action which spawns confusion, more problems, and adds to insecurity.

The conceptual and practical disunity of effort has caused a constant tension between international and domestic actors in Afghanistan. Tension between NATO allies, particularly between the United States and Europeans, peaked in January 2008 when US Defence Secretary, Robert Gates criticised NATO forces of being unprepared for waging counter-insurgency war against the Taliban in Afghanistan. Similarly, President Hamid Karzai has repeatedly disapproved of the allied operations against the Taliban fighters and the use of air bombardment.[18] Diverging views on using tribal militia in fighting insurgents in the south are another case of disagreement. US officials have criticised British-backed plans to arm local militias in an attempt to defeat the Taliban.[19] Traditionally, tribal forces have contributed to local security only under a stronger central government. In unstable conditions they often promoted the spread of warlordism.

17. Aziz Ahmad Shafe in Helmand and Jean MacKenzie in Kabul, Institute for War and Peace Reporting, ARR No. 279, 17 January 2008.

18. White, Griff (2007). "Karzai Decries Civilian Deaths", *Washington Post*, 24 June.

19. Starkey, Jerome (2008). "US attacks UK plans to arm Afghan militias", *The Independent*, UK, 23 January. Also see Dreazen, Yochi J. (2008). "Britain Sees Role for Afghan Tribes", *Wall Street Journal*, 10 January.

Negotiation with the insurgents has not been integrated into an overall strategy but pursued separately by different actors. Although there is wide support for peace talks with insurgents, there is little agreement among domestic and international actors on who to engage, what political price is acceptable in peace deals, and what is the vision for the end state. A British-led deal with the Taliban in September 2006 under which tribal elders took control and agreed to keep the Taliban out, caused tension between NATO and the Afghan government, and raised questions within the alliance. The rebels returned in February and set up a shadow government with their own administrators, courts and officials before they were expelled by a coalition military operation in December 2007. Later the same month, two diplomats accused of holding talks with Taliban militants, allegedly without the knowledge of Afghan authorities, were expelled by the government.[20]

There is growing suspicion in Afghanistan that certain members of the alliance favour a "colonial approach" to gain peace with the Taliban in the South. The approach allegedly entails granting local autonomy to reconciled Taliban leaders who will run local affairs but remain politically loyal to Kabul. This is seen as the creation of an Afghan "FATA" or "Taliban light" enclaves. Such arrangements are doomed to failure for good reasons. First, available opinion surveys indicate that despite the rise of violence, an overwhelming majority of the people view the Taliban negatively and do not favour their return to rule even locally.[21] A year ago, the level of Taliban sympathy in the South was estimated only at 11 per cent.[22] There is a strong inverse correlation between the strength of the government presence and the strength of support for the Taliban.[23] Second, the Pashtuns in

20. Semple, Michael (2007). an Irish EU official with extensive Taliban contacts, and Mervyn Patterson, a UN official from Northern Ireland, travelled to Musa Qala to meet Afghan powerbrokers days after Taliban fighters were driven out by British troops. *Times Online*, "Diplomats Expelled Over Talks with Taleban", 27 December.

21. *Afghan Public Opinion Amidst Rising Violence*, a *WorldPublicOpinion.org* Poll (14 December 2006), fielded by D3 Systems and Afghan Centre for Social and Opinion Research in Kabul, pp. 2–3.

22. Charney Research and ABC News Poll (October 2006), cited in USIP Briefing, *Hearts and Minds: Afghans Opinion on the Taliban, the Government and the International Forces*, 16 August 2007, at <*www.usip.org/usipeace_briefing/2007/0816_Afghan_opinion.html*>

23. Ibid.

Afghanistan are integrated into a multi-ethnic nation that has shown surprising strength and viability with no trace of calls, threats or attempts at secession. Even during the recent civil war and the breakdown of the Central government, the fighting factions were not interested in separatism but were fighting to gain control over Afghanistan. Third, such an ethnic-based decentralisation could generate a domino effect spreading across the country, including the stable areas, leading to fragmentation of the country. At best it would be a tactical gain, but also an immense strategic loss.

Negotiations with foreign-supported militants who want to overthrow the government and turn Afghanistan into a haven for global terrorism are out of the question. Other insurgents, most of whom are not against the political system as an entity but are opposed to the government can be won over through a continuing process of national reconciliation. This will be possible only if these insurgents can be successfully isolated and protected from the radical elements. As long as instability persists in the south, Kabul will be in a weak position to achieve favourable deals through negotiations.

There is an urgent need for consensus among the domestic and international partners on a unified strategy and campaign plan. Implementation will require a major "surge" of troops, equipment and funds to support a cohesive, long-term, integrated military and non-military effort. This may require bringing the NATO-ISAF and US-led Operation Enduring Freedom forces under a unified command with full capacity for both combat operations and stabilisation-peacekeeping efforts. The presence of three major chains of command for the US and ISAF forces does not promote a coordinated strategy on the ground. But the key is also to legitimise the whole campaign strategy with demonstrable Afghan government ownership.

The appointment of the British diplomat Paddy Ashdown as the new UN envoy to Afghanistan with more coordinating power is partly seen as a way to make up for the chronic lack of a coordinated strategy both in the military sphere and in the area of post-conflict or "in-conflict" reconstruction. However, the challenge is much greater than simply coordinating the international effort. Coordinating the Afghan operations and bringing them in line with a coordinated international effort is the main challenge. It is hardly expected that the new envoy will be able to preside over all international efforts and have influence over government decisions to lead a unified coordinated strategy. Kabul has already voiced concerns that a powerful "super-envoy", particularly one from the former colonial power Britain, might further weaken the image and authority of the Afghan government.[24] The alternative is to make the government the sole owner and coordinator of the overall strategy. However, it is not likely to work until the government acquires the capacity to strategise and coordinate the overall efforts for stabilisation and reconstruction.

A counter-insurgency strategy for Afghanistan is incomplete unless it also encompasses Pakistan, whose tribal border areas have become havens for the Taliban and al-Qaeda. Few insurgencies have survived without haven abroad. The upsurge of religious militancy and violence in Pakistan and the Talibanisation of the Federally Administered Tribal Areas (FATA), with increasing spillover to "settled areas" aggravates the impact of regional influence on Afghan developments. The Taliban have havens in Pakistan, and receive technical and operational assistance from transnational extremists there.

The environment in the Pashtun belt has created psychological and political capital for the Taliban and transnational militants. Traditionally a moderate society, the Pashtuns have been more than once radicalised by outside influence and intervention in the past. Most recently, the empowerment of extremist elements by the Pakistani military and intelligence services, and their extensive support for the Taliban in Afghanistan during the 1990s, marginalised moderate political leaders and tribal chiefs in the region. Pakistan's failure to deal with an expanding extremism in the tribal areas and the lack of Afghan government presence in the Pashtun south and south-east have facilitated the rising dominance of extremist elements today.

Removal of sources of insurgency in the area requires a new regional approach involving combined military and political effort by the US, NATO, Afghanistan, and Pakistan. The new approach should address several issues to include the legitimate concerns of both

24. Reuter (2008). "Karzai Seeks U.N. Clarity On Ashdown's Afghan Role", Kabul, 21 January.

Afghanistan and Pakistan, development of the least educated and rural tribal areas on both sides of the Durand Line, promotion of democratic changes in Pakistan, enhancement of governance capacity in Afghanistan, and political integration of FATA. In a larger picture, reducing the sources of transnational militancy and religious extremism in South Asia and economic integration in the region needs to be part of the new approach.

Conclusion

To stop and reverse the negative trends, Afghanistan and its international partners need to make a thorough and realistic assessment of the situation and adopt a strategic action plan to achieve immediate and long-term goals. The strategy should clearly envisage the end state.

Given the compounded political and security situations, no minor, inconsequential changes will save the situation. Major political and strategic shifts, both at the national and international levels, are required now in order to secure Afghanistan's future. The strategy needs to be built on a consensus of domestic and international actors, for effective use of ways and means in achieving peace and stability. Implementation will require a "surge" of capacity, both nationally and internationally.

The foremost requirement is regaining the trust of the people in government and its foreign supporters. This cannot be achieved without a major capacity surge within the government to establish the rule of law, provide human security, and deliver services. Guaranteeing the centrality of the state in governance and reconstruction is essential for enhancing legitimacy of the government. Afghanistan needs to be considered as the "supported partner" while the other actors need to assume a supporting role. The Afghanistan National Development Strategy is being overtaken by events and it needs to be revised into a 5-10-year integrated stabilisation and development strategic plan.

Defeating the insurgency is closely linked with the state-building process and governance in Afghanistan, as well as efforts to address militancy in the region. Unless dramatic actions are taken, the situation could rapidly spiral out of control. Delays in response on the part of allies and regional partners will only compound the myriad of challenges facing Afghanistan: the expansion of militancy in Pakistan, the possible transfer of jihadists to South Asia following the reduction of US forces in Iraq, and various uncertainties associated with Iran.

3

Reconstructing Afghanistan

ANITA INDER SINGH

Anti-terrorism and reconstruction are intertwined tasks of the international players in Afghanistan. This chapter will examine the link between NATO's aims in Afghanistan and America's global anti-terrorist strategy. What problems have had to be faced? What is the strategy and how well is it working? What needs to be done to enhance legitimacy and build stable institutions in Afghanistan? What is the role of international intervention in shaping the future of Afghanistan?

A War on Many Fronts

Afghanistan is the frontline state against terrorism. But after the fall of the Taliban government in 2001 " international intervention" in the country has involved fighting a war on many related fronts. Anti-extremism remains the top priority of the Afghan government and NATO/ISAF. Taliban operations increased by 17 per cent in 2007. Taliban violence in 2008 was at least 30 per cent more than in 2007. Violent incidents went up from 44 a month in 2003 to 573 in 2008, and more than 4500 people were killed after January 2007. In June and July 2008 the US lost more troops in Afghanistan than in Iraq. All this points to a deteriorating security situation, caused by a flawed anti-terrorism strategy.

Meanwhile, the Afghan state, legitimised through presidential and parliamentary elections in 2004 and 2005 respectively, has yet to establish a monopoly of force on its territory. The warlords, many of whom joined forces with the US to overthrow the Taliban, now seek to consolidate their personal fiefs. The growing opium economy is another problem that weakens the authority of the Centre.

Character of Conflict

This is the largest multinational campaign fought by NATO, but there is little coordination between NATO countries or between NATO and Kabul. Washington and its EU allies have different concepts of "strategy".[1] For the US, war is an all-out military campaign. For Europe, which had not seen any wars between 1945 and the 1991 wars in the former Yugoslavia, and which does not wish to spend too much on defence, war is undesirable and morally reprehensible. Secondly, the EU expects the US to bear greater responsibility militarily and financially although its economy is as large as America's. Coordination is unlikely to improve, with reports of mutual dissatisfaction between the US and its NATO allies. A related problem is that the EU itself is divided and does not have a common foreign and defence policy. Whether Kai Eide, the seasoned Norwegian diplomat appointed as the UN Secretary-General's Special Representative in March 2008,[2] has been able to improve coordination between NATO member-states, UNAMA and the government of President Hamid Karzai, is an open question.

Foreigners determine military strategy, not Kabul, because they are providing the men and the money, and training the Afghan National Army (ANA).[3] They decide how the resources will be used. But no one knows how the money is spent: the expenditure is not monitored. Western countries make deals with contractors, not the government. Forty per cent of the aid intended for Afghanistan is returned to donors in the form of payments to Western consultants and others providing services.[4] Afghanistan is also ill served by poor governance, marked by corruption and an ineffective judicial system,[5] which are partly a result of three decades of conflict.

1. Coker, Christopher (2006). "Between Iraq and a Hard Place: Multinational Co-operation, Afghanistan and Strategic Culture", *RUSI Journal* 151(5) (Oct.). See also Bhadrakumar, M.K. (2003). "A New Journey in Search of the Taliban", *The Hindu*, 23 January.
2. *<http://www.unama-afg.org/_latestnews/2008/08march28-press-releasepdf.pdf>*
3. Sky, Emma (2006). "The Lead Nation Approach: The Case of Afghanistan", *RUSI Journal* 151(6) (December).
4. *<http://www.oxfam.org/en/policy/briefingnotes/ACBAR_aid_effectiveness_paper_0803>*
5. *<http://209.85.175.104/search?q=cache:FOP9iSsHKisJ:unpan1.un.org/intradoc/groups/public/documents/APCITY/UNPAN016655.pdf+rama+mani+afghanistan+judiciary &hl=en&ct=clnk&cd=9>*. See also Jones, Seth (2007). "The State of the Afghan Insurgency", *RAND Paper*, CT-296, Testimony presented before the Canadian Senate National Security and Defence Committee on 10 December.

Guns and Development go Hand-in-Hand

NATO's presence in Afghanistan signifies the extension of Europe's security frontier to South Asia. The expansion of NATO's operations in Afghanistan comes in the wake of America's failure to stabilise the country. Almost eight years later the war against the Taliban militants continues. Checking the rising spiral of violence in southern and eastern Afghanistan is a prerequisite for helping Karzai's government to extend its sway over the whole of Afghanistan, building stable institutions of governance, disarmament, demobilisation, and developing capacity for economic development. How long this will take is anybody's guess: Des Browne, the British defence secretary, has said that more British troops would be needed in Afghanistan for decades,[6] and the US is aware that the Afghan campaign will be a long haul.

The Pakistan factor contributes to insecurity. UN, NATO and Afghan officials regard Pakistan as the springboard of renewed Taliban violence. In other words, NATO and Musharraf's Pakistan were allies in the war in Afghanistan even while having conflicting goals.[7] It is curious that the evidence provided by NATO and UN officials of Pakistan's terrorist-training activities did not dissuade George Bush, Tony Blair, and Gordon Brown from continually lauding General Musharraf as a steadfast ally. Since 2001, the US has bestowed more than $10 billion on Pakistan to defeat terrorism, but there is no sign that this aim is being achieved. Most of the largesse is invested in anything from private houses and golf courses for Pakistan's military to shoring up their interests in the hotel industry and cereal factories.[8]

Dismayed at the foundering military campaign in Afghanistan, Congress has raised some questions. Soon after Musharraf's declaration of emergency in November 2007, Congress withheld $50 million of the $300 million aid requested by the Bush administration for Pakistan until Musharraf had restored civil liberties. The remaining $250 million, Congress stipulated, could be used only to fight terrorism, al-Qaeda and the Taliban. But Musharraf took his American

6. *<http://uk.reuters.com/article/topNews/idUKL1346879120080113?rpc=401&>*

7. Tellis, Ashley J. (2008). *Pakistan and the War on Terror: Conflicted Goals, Compromised Performance.* Washington DC: Carnegie Endowment for International Peace.

8. Siddiqa, Ayesha (2007). *Military Inc.: Inside Pakistan's Military Economy.* London: Pluto.

donors by surprise. He told them that the fight was against the Taliban, not al-Qaeda.[9] The Bush White House never responded to his assertion.

Faced with Pakistan's failure to stem the flow of terrorists across the Durand Line, the Bush administration started bombing Pakistan's tribal areas in September 2008, and put pressure on the elected government led by Prime Minister Yusuf Gilani to hunt down the terrorists. A spate of terrorist attacks within Pakistan appears to have persuaded the Gilani government and the post-Musharraf army, headed by General Ashfaq Kiyani, to combat militants in the Bajaur area of north-western Pakistan. Despite claims that hundreds of militants had been killed there, by December 2008, there was not much sign that Islamabad had established control over the region. Clearly, the US and Pakistan may be fighting for different things. But Washington has yet to grasp the nettle.[10]

In his speech to the opening session of the Afghan parliament on 21 January 2008, President Karzai remarked that the threat of terrorism in Afghanistan stemmed from both inside and outside the country and the broad strategy of "targeting its original sources, drying up its financial sources, and stopping the expansion of extremism must be included as the key points in the fight on terrorism". Karzai's mention of the "original source" of terrorism was widely interpreted as a reference to Pakistan. He stressed the necessity of putting an end to terrorist sanctuaries in Pakistan again in November 2008.[11]

With the rout of the Taliban, Afghanistan needed peace-building, a euphemistic term coined by former UN Secretary-General Boutros Boutros-Ghali[12] for building a new state from scratch. Some $27.5 billion were needed for the reconstruction of Afghanistan.[13] From the

---

9. Tellis, Pakistan *and the War on Terror,* n.7, pp.38–9.

10. Singh, Anita Inder (2008). "With friends like Musharraf", 12 March, <*http://commentisfree.guardian.co.uk/anita_inder_singh/2008/02/with_friends_like_musharraf_.html*>

11. <*http://www.guardian.co.uk/commentisfree/2008/nov/13/afghanistan-terrorism-al-qaida*>

12. *An Agenda for Peace,* Second Edition. New York: United Nations, 1995.

13. *Securing Afghanistan's Future: Accomplishments and the Strategic Path Forward,* 17 March 2004; prepared by the Afghan government and international agencies for the International Conference at Berlin, 31 March–1 April 2004.

outset it was clear that America's military and economic strength would make it a key player in post-war Afghanistan. The US had two choices: to work for a stable democratic Afghanistan, or one that might be less than ideally democratic but might promote development.[14] Development could not take place without a semblance of democracy, and neither could be achieved without security. Security was America's top priority from the outset. Reconstruction required a kind of Marshall Aid Plan for Afghanistan, but there was none. Nor did the US want to have charge of governing Afghanistan. Bush affirmed, on 25 September 2001, that the US would steer clear of nation-building in Afghanistan. Washington's wish to limit its engagement in Afghanistan was in contrast to American strategies after the defeat of Germany and Japan at the end of World War II. In Germany, American military and civilian personnel restored institutions of local governance, ran everyday administration, distributed food, organised transport and health care. American soldiers were taught how to disarm the local police and to interact with the local population. In both Germany and Japan, the US was willing to station troops over an extended period; in fact they remained for seven years. The US garrisons controlled the whole of Japan, and along with their British and French allies, three out of four military sectors in Germany.[15]

To some extent, the American shortfall in Afghanistan is a consequence of American entanglements in Iraq since 2003. Although Afghanistan is at the forefront of Washington's "global war on terror" and has a larger population (32 million) than Iraq (28 million), Iraq has received the lion's share of the money disbursed by the Bush administration to protect national security. From 2001 to 2009, the US allocated $171.1 billion for Afghanistan, compared to $653.1 billion for Iraq. The average expenditure on Afghanistan per year has been $21.46 billion; $108.9 billion for Iraq.[16]

---

14. "Afghanistan and the Challenge of Reconstruction", 17 January 2002, at <*www.ceip.org*>
15. Jennings, Ray Salvatore (2003). The *Road Ahead: Lessons in Nation Building from Japan, Germany, and Afghanistan for Postwar Iraq*. Washington DC: United States Institute of Peace. April. pp.27–9.
16. Singh, Anita Inder (n.d.). "Obama's Afghan Challenge", at <*http://www.opendemocracy.net/terrorism/article/anita_indersingh/obama_afghanistan_challenge*>

Of the estimated $27.5 billion needed to rebuild Afghanistan the US pledged $296 million in 2002, the EU and Japan $500 million each, India and Pakistan $100 million each, Iran $560 million, and Saudi Arabia $220 million. Of the $4560 billion aid allocated in 2002 by the US, only $90 million was given to Karzai's government to support its activities. But by mid-2003 the US had made up these deficiencies as part of the $87 billion aid package for Iraq and Afghanistan. Most of the aid—some 80 per cent—was spent on relief programmes rather than reconstruction.[17]

No accurate account exists of the amount of aid committed to and spent on reconstruction.[18] But the US seems to be putting in a lot more than the EU. Of the €7.09 billion offered by the international community by 2011, €2.7 billion was given by the US. At the Tokyo conference, the European Commission pledged €1 billion in reconstruction aid over five years (2002-2006). Since then, the Commission has provided over €657 million to Afghanistan in reconstruction aid. The allocation for 2007-2010 is € 610 million. The UK alone, Afghanistan's second-largest donor, pledged €598 million over three years. This is very little compared to EU contributions to other war-torn countries. A RAND study shows that Afghanistan received €38.5 per capita in the first two years of assistance, while Bosnia received €458.6, East Timor €157, and Haiti €50.

While the European Commission expects to deliver €560 million over four years in Afghanistan, the US administration has requested an additional €900 million for reconstruction, governance, and humanitarian activities from Congress for 2008 alone. According to RAND, the US is spending

> seven times the resources to counter-narcotics activities provided by the United Kingdom (leading counter-narcotics campaign), nearly 50 times the resources to the police provided by Germany (leading police reform), and virtually everything for training the Afghan military (for which the United States was responsible).

---

17. "The United States and the Global Coalition Against Terrorism, September 2001–December 2003, entry for 21 January 2002.

18. This section is based on Nixon, Hamish (2007). "Aiding the State? International Assistance and the Statebuilding Paradox in Afghanistan", *AREU Briefing Paper*, April; "International Community Pledging Outcomes", London Conference on Afghanistan, 1 February 2006, at <*www.fco.gov.uk*>, accessed 30 July 2007; and Dobbins, James Seth G. Jones, Keith Crane, Andrew Rathmell, Brett Steele, Richard Teltschik, and Anga Timilsina (2005). *The UN's Role in Nation-Building: From the Congo to Iraq*. Santa Monica CA: RAND. p.xxii.

France's pledge of €37 million over five years is less than that of the UK, Germany, Spain, the Netherlands, Denmark, Sweden, and Finland. This is particularly striking when set against France's overall development budget of €7.84 billion in 2007, representing 0.42 per cent of GNP. What is more, the EU does not set its priorities efficiently, and ends up spending money on projects that do not contribute significantly to Afghanistan's reconstruction. As the largest donor, Washington, not the EU, has the most leverage over any government in Kabul and over its allies.

Anti-terrorist Allies—A Double-edged Sword

Since 2001, the long-term American strategy of forging security sometimes seems to be at odds with its tactics and choice of allies. Necessity compelled the US to combine with the Northern Alliance to defeat the Taliban; neither the Americans nor the Alliance could have achieved that on their own. For the warlords, too, expediency forged the anti-Taliban compact. In siding with the US they were not motivated by the desire to consolidate security, let alone introduce democracy. In 2001, the power vacuum after the defeat of the Taliban gave the warlords the chance to carve out personal fiefdoms and, at times, America's "post-Taliban" collaboration with them only seemed to increase instability.

Afghanistan is divided into 34 provinces,[19] which are subdivided into *hauzas*. The *hauzas*, created by the Soviets, formed the bases of the warlords, who exercised a combination of military, political and economic power outside any constitutional framework. Historically, the Central government had been weak in Afghanistan. With the help of Pakistan's intelligence services, the US fought the Soviets by giving arms and money to several Afghan military commanders, thereby facilitating the rise of warlordism. After the events of 11 September 2001, Pakistan was America's conduit to the warlords. So the warlords continued to fight for territory and power, not just against the Taliban. Perhaps fearful that they might lose power after the October 2004

19. On 5 June 2004, two new provinces were created by presidential decree to delineate provincial electoral boundaries before the elections to be held in October 2004. Report of the Secretary-General, *The Situation in Afghanistan and Its Implications for International Peace and Security*, A/58/868–S/2004/634, 12 August 2004, para. 10.

elections, perhaps hoping to use the elections as a chance to preserve or expand their own political base, strong military leaders within and outside the government of Hamid Karzai jostled to secure a political vantage point through military means, perpetuating instability in the country.

The warlords also had economic reasons to create their own fiefs. Afghanistan produces more than 90 per cent of the world's opium.[20] Half of Afghanistan's GNP is earned through the opium trade. The end of the Taliban government saw an increase in the growth of poppies in the areas controlled by the warlords, even as they helped the US to hunt Osama bin Laden, and members of al-Qaeda and the Taliban. Apparently, the Bush administration turned a blind eye to the involvement of its warlord friends in local wars and the narcotics trade. The production of opium poppies filled their coffers with the cash to buy weapons: their annual income from this was estimated at about $2.3 billion, or almost eight times the government's tax revenues. Indeed, opium production increased by 17 per cent in 2007 over 2006.[21]

Much of the opium produced in Afghanistan ends up in Europe, through Central Asia and the Caucasus, including Chechnya. Ninety per cent of the heroin that makes its way into Britain comes from Afghanistan. Within Afghanistan, the warlords control the routes through which the opium is transported to foreign countries. These routes are also used for cross-border infiltration by terrorists financed by Saudi Arabia and trained by Pakistan. The warlords control the major customs posts, including Kandahar, Herat, Jalalabad, and Balkh, through which goods are smuggled into Pakistan. They have strengthened their authority through smuggling, trafficking in drugs, and illegal transit fees.

---

20. *<http://www.un.org/apps/news/story.asp?NewsID=23597&Cr=afghan&Cr1>; <http://www.unodc.org/afg/news_and_events_2007-06-25.html>*

21. *<http://209.85.175.104/search?q=cache:XFrVVf-FJv0J:www.unodc.org/pdf/research/AFG07_ExSum_web.pdf+opium+production+in+afghanistan+2007&hl=en&ct=clnk&cd=1>*

Demobilisation, Disarmament, and Reconstruction Problems

President Hamid Karzai's first task was to stabilise the country,[22] but his writ has never run outside Kabul. The US appears to have kept a foot in both camps: supporting Karzai but helping—or at least overlooking—the belligerence of the warlords. To capture members of the Taliban the US worked with the warlords, including Abdul Rashid Dostum, Ismail Khan, the governor of Herat, and Gul Agha Sherzai, the governor of Kandahar, all of whom had their own foot-soldiers. Ismail Khan headed a militia of some 30,000 and controlled lucrative customs posts on the borders with Iran and Turkmenistan. In August 2003, he refused to disband his private armed force or step down as provincial military commander under a rule that he could not concurrently hold a civil and a military position.

The complexities and contradictions inherent in this strategy were evident before the October 2004 presidential elections. Many warlords challenged the authority of Karzai, whom the Bush administration wished to see elected as president. Karzai himself vowed not to include recalcitrant warlords in a post-election government if he were elected president. But giving them the sack could provoke turbulence. Seeking to expand his authority over the country before polling day on 9 October, Karzai ousted Ismail Khan on 12 September as governor of Herat. His boldness triggered a spate of violence, including an attack on the local UN office, after which the UN personnel left the city. Prior to the elections, Karzai had to negotiate with the warlords. The dialogue continued after his electoral victory.

The results of these messy compromises with truculent, feuding warlords were clear after the elections as well: security remained the greatest challenge to the emergence of peace, democratic processes, and stability. The problem was not confined to military issues: it extended to the narcotics trade, border and customs control, structural economic reforms, and building roads in Afghanistan and to neighbouring states. Insecurity meant that foreign countries would be reluctant to invest in Afghanistan. The US was unwilling to be mired, "Vietnam style", in Afghanistan. But by colluding with both the Karzai and

22. This discussion is based on Singh, Anita Inder (2006). *The United States, South Asia and the Global Anti-Terrorist Coalition*. New Delhi. pp.22–6.

warlord camps, the US actually worked against inclusive democracy and stability that it sought in Afghanistan.

Reconstruction: Divisions in the Government and Local Factors

There was infighting in the government between reformist and more conservative ministers. This sometimes blocked the introduction and implementation of political and administrative reform. On 28 January 2002, President Bush committed the US to training a new national army and police force for Afghanistan, but it was several months later, on 2 December 2002, that the Afghan National Army was created by presidential decree. The decree outlawed private militias but the mistrust and rivalry among military commanders stalled demobilisation of their forces and the establishment of a national army.[23] Ethnic differences, combined with the desire for political power, prevented the development of a new army. The fact that the Ministry of Defence was in charge of both the national army and the Afghan militia forces hardly helped. Muhammad Fahim, the Defence Minister, filled the Defence Ministry with fellow Tajiks and kept the strength of the new ANA down to a mere 7500 troops instead of the 40,000 it needed to extend the centre's authority. Fahim also maintained about 30,000 private troops in Kabul and turned down international requests to demobilise them. Barely 5 per cent of his foot-soldiers were disarmed before the election. A plan to train a Pashtun force for military action in southern and eastern Afghanistan, where the Taliban and al-Qaeda are strong, fell through because General Basilar Khan, a Tajik, opposed its formation. Another militia was headed by the Agriculture Minister Sayyid Hussain Anwari. New militia, their strength unknown, were continually created and equipped with new weapons.

The UN wanted 40 per cent of all militia to be disarmed before the elections. This would have involved decommissioning whole divisions. Fahim countered that the size of each militia be reduced by 40 per cent while leaving their structure and the authority of their commanders intact.[24] He would not reduce divisions loyal to him: their strength

23. *Security in Afghanistan*, p.80.

24. "Elections and Security in Afghanistan", International Crisis Group Report, p.3.

increased his standing during the election campaign. Disarmament remained incomplete in December 2004. At one point, an embattled Karzai observed that warlord militia were a bigger problem than the Taliban because they were undermining the building of institutions in the country.[25]

A multi-ethnic force could only be created with outside help. To counter the Tajiks the US set up recruitment centres in Kabul, Jalalabad, Gardez, Banyan, and Kandahar in the hope of building a more ethnically diverse army. But that was not enough: the ANA had a desertion rate of 10 per cent. With the political situation in flux, military commanders were fearful that a national army would reduce their power and were unwilling to surrender arms. The strength of the militia hostile to Karzai was unknown—it could have been as high as 90,000.[26] Internecine struggles within groups or between warlords have exacerbated tensions.

In 2008, the ANA had about 80,000 troops. With Barack Obama calling for a surge of about 20,000 American troops before he took over as President in January 2009, the inference is that NATO forces will have to stay in Afghanistan for a considerable time to come. But some NATO countries, such as Germany and the Netherlands, wish to withdraw from the battlefield, at a time when Taliban violence has increased[27] and more rather than less troops would be needed. The 3000 additional American troops sent to Afghanistan in April 2008 and the 700 committed by France at the Bucharest Summit would not suffice to make up the troop shortfall. The long-term solution is to enlarge and accelerate the training of the ANA.

NATO's failure to establish its own garrisons throughout the country reflects its failure to dismantle the competing militia or to build a viable national army under the Central government's command. The Japanese funded a project to disarm, demobilise, and reintegrate about 40 per cent of the Northern Alliance forces that

25. Rashid, Ahmed (2004). "A Vote is Cast Against the Warlords", *Far Eastern Economic Review*, 29 July, and Richburg, Keith (2004). "Karzai Vows to Crack Down on Warlords, Drug Dealers", *The Washington Post*, 5 November.

26. O'Hanlon, Michael (2004). "Let's Finish the Job in Afghanistan", *The Baltimore Sun*, 13 October.

27. <*http://ap.google.com/article/ALeqM5g6zVz-oQ-fvGQDXykx-ozLJSdUjwD8VTJV581*>

helped America to defeat the Taliban. But on account of the low level of incentives offered to the militiamen to give up their weapons and to disband their troops, the programme fizzled out.

The Afghan security and police forces are inadequate in numbers and deficient in professionalism. The training of the national police is lagging behind. In May 2007, it was decided to increase the police target to 82,000, to include 18,000 Border Police.

Glimmer of Hope

Did Karzai's election as President in 2004 strengthen the democratic forces? The acceptance of the election results by his militarised opponents suggested a willingness, no matter how tentative, to play by the first rule of the democratic game. Qanuni's decision to form a political party to contest the parliamentary elections in 2005 mirrors at least a willingness to try to gain power through the ballot box rather than through guns.

Nevertheless, security will remain at the top of the political and military agendas—for Karzai and for the US—and it will be among the toughest challenges facing the new American administration after January 2009. Whether in 2004, 2005 or 2009, elections could not be an exit strategy for the US. Rather, Washington must increase military and economic aid to Karzai to strengthen his position, to have more carrots—and if necessary sticks—to negotiate and bargain successfully after the elections, to make the political dialogue among Afghan politicians as constructive as possible. Karzai will need military support to contain warlordism and to sustain the process of peace-building that has been given a fillip by the presidential elections.

Dealing with Ethnic and Tribal Divisions

Karzai simultaneously has to overcome and work with the tribal divisions among his cabinet colleagues. He must counter the possibility of Pakistan exploiting any discontent among the Pashtuns. Islamabad harped on the theme that they had lost out after 9/11 and that Pakistan wanted to help them. That propaganda made little impression on the Pashtuns in Afghanistan, who made no moves for cross-border Pashtun unity—which worked to Karzai's advantage.

Karzai won in the areas bordering Pakistan, including Kandahar, Kabul, Paktika, and other border provinces which had been the stronghold of warlords, including Herat, Balkh, and Kunduz. He won more than 90 per cent of the votes in many Pashtun provinces, 60 per cent in Wardak, and 53 per cent in Ghazni, which extend into Hazara areas. In mixed areas such as Farsawan and Herat his margin was lower but he still obtained the majority of votes. Qanuni, his main rival, failed to consolidate his base among his own Tajik community. In the Tajik-majority province of Badakshan, Karzai won more than half the votes.

But Karzai will still have to win over the Hazaras in the central highlands and also in Kabul. A large share of the Uzbek vote went to Ahmad Rashid Dostum. Uzbeks and Tajiks now control areas once dominated by the Taliban.

The outstanding reality is that Karzai must build a new political and economic infrastructure that will lay the foundations of long-term peace and development in Afghanistan. He must persuade the warlords to transfer power to his elected government, build up a national army and police force. The illegal armed groups must be demobilised and a healthy civil society developed. The success of state-building in Afghanistan is necessary for the containment, if not the defeat, of terrorism there.

The Challenges Remain

- The government and its provincial outposts must convince the Afghans that the state is legitimate, representative, and effective enough to provide at least some basic services in addition to security, law, and order.
- Delivery has been hampered by the contradictory policies of the national, local, and international bodies. The provincial reconstruction teams (PRTs), UNAMA, Special Forces, all compete to implement local development projects. But short-term projects, focusing on security—distributed by the military and aimed at building consent through creating physical assets—often conflict with longer-term UN-supported government projects and processes.

- There are currently about 25 PRTs, which comprise civilian and military personnel. Their mandate includes security, support to the Central government, reconstruction, and security sector reform. They are concerned with state-building but they require cooperation from the local actors. Their aims have often been at odds with those of the local tribal leaders and military commanders. They depend on the military for essentials such as transport. But the military tend to focus more on short-term tactics rather than the achievement of long-term objectives such as reconstruction.

  The weakness of the Afghan centre, and Kabul's limited reach, which hardly extends outside Kabul, have in fact enabled the PRTs to replace the state that they are supposed to be building. They have also tended to undermine the status of the local dignitaries, whose support could help their local projects succeed.[28]

- A multiplicity of models of local governance—including traditional structures such as *shuras*, community development councils (CDCs), and the formal institutions—complicate delivery and give militia commanders clout against the government and to intimidate the citizens.
- The ministries need to be decentralised in their functioning for more efficient delivery of most key services in the country. The Directorate for Local Governance and some central ministries such as the Ministry for Education have delegated tasks such as teacher recruitment to the provincial level. These attempts to strengthen local governance must be sustained by the donors.
- Police training needs to be improved; pay and facilities increased. The combination of war and poor communications results in existing police posts not being supplied with basic necessities like food, heating fuel, and water.
- The deteriorating security environment shows that the strategy needs a review. For instance, NATO forces withdraw from a

28. Yaqub, Daoud and William Maley (2008). "NATO and Afghanistan: Saving the State-Building Enterprise", *The Bucharest Papers*. London: Chatham House.

place immediately after defeating the Taliban—leaving the door open for them to return.

- Unprotected by NATO or the ANA, ordinary Afghans make deals with the Taliban in order simply to survive.
- NATO and Karzai are divided on whether to engage in dialogue with the Taliban. NATO's capture of Musa Qala on 12 December 2007 was facilitated because some Taliban switched allegiance. Talking to the Taliban therefore, seems an essential part of the strategy. But Karzai and NATO have different ideas about whom they should talk to. The recent expulsion of two UN officials who had started a dialogue with the Taliban highlighted this.
- NATO must review the Pakistan strand of its strategy. Pakistan was mentioned in the Bucharest communiqué under "regional approaches"; but the communiqué provided no clue of how Islamabad will be tackled. The omens are not particularly encouraging. Much to Washington's dismay, the elected government of Yusuf Raza Gilani seeks to engage in dialogue with militants in the FATA.[29] The crucial question is the attitude of the military and intelligence services (MIS), which have trained the extremists since long. The army could not reasonably back dialogue while continuing to train extremists and exporting them to Afghanistan. On the other hand, extremists have recently[30] inflicted several defeats on Pakistani soldiers—and the high command cannot be insensitive to morale in the rank and file of the army. So it is anyone's guess how the "intensified dialogue" with Pakistan, anticipated by the Bucharest Declaration, would make Afghanistan safe from terrorism. Since September 2008, American missile attacks in north-west Pakistan have violated Pakistan's sovereignty, and angered the country's civilian and military establishment. Efforts by Gilani's government and Kiyani's army to crush terrorists in the north-western tribal areas have yet to achieve a breakthrough—and there is no consensus in Pakistan's parliament on the necessity

29. <*http://www.nytimes.com/2008/03/22/world/asia/22pstan.html?partner=rssnyt&emc=rss&pagewanted=print*>

30. <*http://www.timesonline.co.uk/tol/comment/columnists/guest_contributors/article5092906.ece*>

of military action against the extremists who threaten the country's own security. There is no sign that Washington will dump Pakistan as an ally if it continues to foster extremism.[31]

- As regards reconstruction, the EU prefers soft to hard power[32] and wants to train the police. But the police are no match for the increasing numbers of Taliban fighters coming across the border from Pakistan. American hard power was and remains necessary to rout the Taliban—but a poorly coordinated strategy is not working against them.

  Even if some EU countries do not wish to send more soldiers to the battlefield they could still make a significant contribution to stabilising Afghanistan. They could do what Europe is good at—preparing the ground for economic betterment through aid. That means, among other things, developing Afghanistan's economy so that its opium-growing farmers, comprising 14 per cent of the population, are presented with alternative sources of livelihood. Financially ruined by three decades of war, they can hardly be persuaded to give up opium cultivation when one hectare of poppies earns them ten times what one hectare of wheat earns.

  True, an ever higher price will have to be paid to stamp out the Taliban. For instance, the costs borne by Britain have soared by 122 per cent since 2001, largely to buy better materiel. Yet even 1.6 billion being spent on this account is inadequate: British troops in Afghanistan are under-funded and ill equipped.[33]

- More generally, EU soft power is not working either. One possible explanation is that even soft power has to be sustained by money, and the slow progress in security and reconstruction suggests that the EU could do more. Three facts stand out. First, the EU's economy is as large as that of the US; secondly, the world spends a trillion dollars on defence every year; thirdly, 90 per cent of that expenditure is by Western countries. If the EU

31. As suggested by Kurlantzick, Joshua (2007), "Time's Up: The US Needs to Abandon Musharraf Today", New Republic, 5 November, at <*http://www.tnr.com/politics/story.html?id=ec9a1aa2-db80-46f0-abf4-c04388c80f8d*>

32. <*http://yaleglobal.yale.edu/display.article?id=7059*>

33. <*http://www.guardian.co.uk/uk/2008/mar/11/military.iraq*>

believes in the benefits of soft power is it willing to spend as much on its use and maintenance as the US spends on hard power? It is a question of the EU practising what it preaches. Instead of cutting down aid, the EU should reverse the decline of the last few years and contribute more. Security and reconstruction are proceeding at a snail's pace in Afghanistan, underlining the need for greater largesse to Afghanistan, especially by the EU, which contributes far less than America to military or state-building efforts.[34]

In Afghanistan, the EU has the unparalleled opportunity to show the world that soft power can create lasting peace and enhance human security.

The ANA will increasingly take the lead in military operations. This is desirable, because it would be more familiar with Afghanistan's people and terrain than NATO soldiers. NATO's role would gradually become that of a trainer and mentor. But neither that nor the deployment of 20-30,000 American and 700 French troops[35] would ensure NATO's success against extremists.

- NATO will continue to have a rough ride in Afghanistan in the foreseeable future. Only if Eide is able to persuade the West to increase troop strength and funding, unite all anti-extremist parties, including NATO, UNAMA,[36] the EU and the Karzai government, will the vision of a secure, terrorism-free and democratic Afghanistan be realised.
- On the optimistic side, the Taliban are not a mass movement. The Afghans do not want to be ruled again by them. But extremists cannot make headway without some measure of popular support or connivance. They seem to be in a position to obstruct every reconstruction or political strategy at every step.

34. *<http://www.washingtonpost.com/wpdyn/content/article/2007/10/05/AR2007100501041_pf.html>*; Singh, Anita Inder (2008). "Bankrolling Kabul", *The Guardian* 12 March, *<http://commentisfree.guardian.co.uk/anita_inder_singh/2008/03/bankrolling_kabul.html>*

35. *<http://www.rferl.org/featuresarticle/2008/04/8e6f1eb7-bb63-44a4-a0a1-6fe78c652d6f.html>*

36. *<http://www.unama-afg.org/>*

This is where the hearts-and-minds approach matters.[37] People want security—in the end the Taliban cannot give it to them. The crucial question is whether the US and EU are merely seeking an exit strategy of failure or are ready to raise the resources to stay the course and defeat terrorism in Afghanistan. Generosity to Afghanistan would well turn out to be pragmatic politics.

- In 2009, the US may deploy another 15,000 to 20,000 troops in Afghanistan, a strategy reportedly favoured by Obama.[38] Any increase in troop strength must be accompanied by more money both to fight the militants and carry out reconstruction. As Admiral Mike Mullen,[39] Chairman of the US Joint Chiefs of Staff told the Congressional Armed Services Committee on 11 September 2008, Afghanistan needs more than just boots on the ground

> [Indent long quote] It needs more trucks on the roads, teachers in schools, trained judges and lawyers in courts, foreign investments, alternative crops, sound governance, the rule of law—these are the keys to success in Afghanistan...We cannot kill our way to victory.

In the twilight of its tenure, the Bush administration could not be a source of strategic rethinking. The challenge facing Barack Obama demands not only renewed commitment but bold imagination to make military and human security a reality in Afghanistan.

---

37. Richards, David (2006). "NATO in Afghanistan: Transformation on the Front Line", *RUSI Journal*, 151(4) (August); RUSI Interview with General David Richards, 152(2) (April 2007).

38. <*http://www.washingtonpost.com/wpdyn/content/article/2008/11/10/AR2008111002897_pf.html*>

39. <*http://english.aljazeera.net/news/americas/2008/09/200891016383687l959.html*>

4

Afghanistan Redux

Countering the Taliban-Led Insurgency

SETH G. JONES

Afghanistan has long been a graveyard of empires. Around 330 BC, Alexander the Great and his army faced some of their fiercest battles and suffered staggering losses against tribes in Afghanistan. In the 19th century, the British fought three brutal wars in Afghanistan to balance Russian influence in the region. The first Anglo–Afghan War, which lasted from 1839 to 1842, ended in a humiliating British defeat. The departing British force, which numbered 16,000 soldiers, was systematically reduced to one as British forces battled through biting cold and knee-deep snow. William Brydon, the only survivor, later recalled: "This was a terrible march, the fire of the enemy incessant, and numbers of officers and men, not knowing where they were going from snow-blindness, were cut up."[1] In 1878, the British invaded again in the second Anglo–Afghan War. The war commenced with a swift invasion by 33,500 British troops on three fronts, but cholera swept through the British ranks, and daytime temperatures in the shade rose to over one hundred degrees Fahrenheit.[2] Despite a decisive victory at the Battle of Kandahar in 1880, the British pulled out, following intense domestic opposition to the war in Britain. The third Anglo–Afghan war began in 1919 and ended later that year with the Treaty of Rawalpindi, which was signed between Britain and Afghan leaders on 8 August 1919, where the British recognised Afghan independence.

The Soviet Union suffered a similar fate. The Soviet invasion of Afghanistan in 1979 was met with fierce resistance from the Afghan

---

1. Lawrence, Sir George (1981). *Reminiscences of Forty-Three Years in India.* Lahore: Sang-e-Meel. pp.308–9. The appendix of the book includes a copy of William Brydon's account of the journey, made on arrival at Jalalabad in 1842.

2. Holt, *Into the Land of Bones*, p.4.

population, and Afghanistan became a graveyard of Russian and mujahideen fighters. Pakistan's Inter-Services Intelligence (ISI) Directorate, with assistance from the US Central Intelligence Agency (CIA) and Saudi intelligence, provided substantial assistance to the mujahideen and such leaders as Gulbuddin Hikmatyar and Jalaluddin Haqqani. Some of these leaders would later take up arms against the United States after the September 2001 terrorist attacks. When the Soviets withdrew in February 1989, the country was devastated. An estimated one million Afghans were killed, more than five million fled abroad, and as many as three million people were internally displaced.[3]

The United States and NATO forces find themselves in a similar position. In 2008, for example, quantitative and qualitative data indicated that there was an increasingly violent insurgency threatening the country. It included a range of insurgent groups, such as the Taliban, the Haqqani network, foreign fighters (including al-Qaeda), Hizb-i-Islami, criminal organisations, and some allied tribes and sub-tribes. Between 2002 and 2006, the number of insurgent-initiated attacks increased by 400 per cent, and the number of deaths from these attacks increased more than 800 per cent.[4] Insurgent-initiated attacks rose another 27 per cent between 2006 and 2007.[5] The result was a lack of security for Afghans and foreigners.

Several provinces around Kabul also became dangerous. In late 2006, I drove by car from Afghanistan's capital city, Kabul, to neighbouring Wardak Province. The two-hour journey meanders through a parched landscape of sedimentary rocks and jagged mountain peaks. In 2008, however, I couldn't repeat the journey. It

3. Rashid, Ahmed (2000). *Taliban: Militant Islam, Oil and Fundamentalism in Central Asia.* New Haven, Conn.: Yale University Press. p.13; Rubin, Barnett R. (1995). *The Search for Peace in Afghanistan: From Buffer State to Failed State.* New Haven, Conn.: Yale University Press. p.7; Grau. *The Bear Went Over the Mountain.* p.xix.

4. Following are the yearly figures on insurgent-initiated attacks in Afghanistan: 2002 (65); 2003 (148); 2004 (146); 2005 (207); and 2006 (353). Following are the fatalities: 2002 (79); 2003 (133); 2004 (230); 2005 (288); and 2006 (755). Data are from the RAND-MIPT Terrorism Incident database. A comparison of the RAND-MIPT data with the US and European government data shows that the RAND-MIPT data significantly understates the number of attacks and deaths because most improvised explosive device and armed attacks were not reported in the press. Nevertheless, the trend in these data is consistent with the US and European government data.

5. The data come from Admiral Michael Mullen, Chairman of the Joint Chiefs of Staff. See, for example, Johnson, Ed (2007). "Gates Wants NATO To Reorganize Afghanistan Mission", *Bloomberg News*, 12 December.

was too dangerous. The Taliban and other insurgent groups infiltrated into Kabul's surrounding provinces. Indeed, provinces that I could drive to only a few months ago, such as Wardak and Lowgar, were off limits except to those willing to gamble with their lives. Insurgent and criminal groups set up checkpoints along major roads to collect taxes and seize stray Westerners or Afghans who supported the central government. Kidnapping had become a growth industry. In southern Afghanistan, the insurgency continued to rage. In Kandahar Province, Canadian, other NATO, and Afghan government forces fought pitched battles with Taliban and insurgent forces. As one senior NATO official told me, NATO and Afghan forces controlled at most 20 per cent of southern Afghanistan in late 2007. The rest was controlled by Taliban or a range of local militia forces.

This chapter asks several interlinked questions. First, why do insurgencies begin? Second, why did Afghanistan's insurgency begin? Third, what are the implications for resolving the insurgency? The chapter begins by outlining what has caused the rise of insurgencies in the past, and then examines the rising insurgency in Afghanistan.

Historical Lessons

Weak and ineffective governance has historically been a necessary precondition for the rise of insurgencies because it creates a supply of disgruntled locals.[6] Governance, as used here, is defined as the set of institutions by which authority in a country is exercised.[7] It includes the ability to establish law and order, effectively manage resources, and implement sound policies. An insurgency reflects a process of alternative state building, where insurgents compete to provide governance to the population. Insurgents take advantage of weak governance and assume state-like functions. They tax, set up administrative structures, and seek to perform government functions for the population they control. As one study concluded:

6. Hironaka, Ann (2005). *Neverending Wars: The International Community, Weak States, and the Perpetuation of Civil War.* Cambridge, Mass.: Harvard University Press; Fearon and Laitin. "Ethnicity, Insurgency, and Civil War", pp.75–90. On the importance of building institutions, see Paris, Roland (2004). *At War's End: Building Peace After Civil Conflict.* New York: Cambridge University Press.
7. World Bank (2006). *Governance Matters 2006: Worldwide Governance Indicators.* Washington DC. p.2.

> Insurgency can best be understood as a process of competitive state building rather than simply an instance of collective action or social contention...State building is the insurgent's central goal and renders organized and sustained rebellion of the kind that takes places in civil wars fundamentally distinct from phenomena such as banditry, mafias, or social movements.[8]

We should expect, then, that the probability of an insurgency increases in states with weak governance.

Logic of Weak Governance

Weak governance significantly increases the possibility of an insurgency. German sociologist Max Weber defined the state as "a human community that (successfully) claims the monopoly of the legitimate use of physical force within a given territory."[9] A key essence of weak governance, then, is enforcement: the government is unable to force people to comply with the state's laws. Weak governance also means that the government is ineffective in managing resources and implementing polices.[10] This can include the poor quality of public services, poor quality of policy formulation and implementation, and little credibility of the government's commitment to such policies. The population has little confidence in the rules of society, including the quality of contract enforcement, the police, and the courts. Corruption is often rampant. Corruption includes the extent to which public power is exercised for private gain, including both petty and grand forms of corruption, as well as capture of the state by elites and private interests, law, and control of corruption.[11]

Philosophers have long noted the link between viable governance and stability.[12] Thomas Hobbes argued, for example, that a critical element in establishing a peaceful, stable society is to confer sovereign authority on one individual or group of individuals, what he called the Leviathan. Hobbes argued that members of society should pledge "not to resist the

---

8. Kalyvas, Stathis N. (2006). *The Logic of Violence in Civil War*. New York: Cambridge University Press. p.218.

9. Weber, Max (1958). "Politics as a Vocation", in H.H. Gerth and C. Wright Mills (eds.), *From Max Weber: Essays in Sociology*. New York: Oxford University Press. p.78.

10. On governance, see Kaufman, Daniel Aart Kraay, and Massimo Mastruzzi (2002). *Governance Matters III: Governance Indicators for 1996–2002*. Washington DC: The World Bank; Kaufmann, Daniel (2005)."Myths and Realities of Governance and Corruption", in *The World Economic Forum, Global Competitiveness Report 2005–06*. Geneva: World Economic Forum. pp.81–98; Paris, *At War's End*.

11. Daniel, Kraay, and Mastruzzi (2001). Ibid.: 4.

12. See the discussion in Paris, *At War's End*, pp.40–51.

commands of that man or council that they have recognized as their sovereign."[13] Even Adam Smith, famous for advocating a minimal government role and arguing that the free market is guided to produce the right amount and variety of goods by a so-called invisible hand, supported a strong and competent security force to establish domestic order. In *The Wealth of Nations,* he noted that "the first duty of the sovereign, that of protecting the society from the violence and invasion of other independent societies, can be performed only by means of a military force."[14] Sovereigns who could not depend on a loyal and effective security force, he asserted, would be more likely to suppress liberty than rulers backed by strong security forces. The reason is straightforward: leaders with the support of the security services would feel safe enough to permit expression of public dissent. Similarly, Immanuel Kant argued that in the absence of the rule of law enforced by a central authority, peaceful coexistence among free individuals would be impossible and would collapse into a "lawless state of savagery."[15] Peace, therefore, required a powerful sovereign. But peace also required a sovereign whose powers were limited to what was necessary to preserve the rule of law. Only by constraining individual liberty through the consistent (and, if necessary, coercive) application of law was it possible to preserve the security and freedom of all.[16]

In the *Federalist Papers*, Alexander Hamilton argued that it was a vital task for the government to maintain domestic and external security. "A firm Union", he wrote, "will be of the utmost moment to the peace and liberty of the states, as a barrier against domestic faction and insurrection" and as a guarantor of "internal tranquillity."[17] He argued that a strong executive branch was especially important to public security and the administration of law, including the protection of individual rights: "A feeble Executive is but another phrase for a bad execution; and a government ill executed, whatever it may be in theory,

13. Berns, Laurence (1987). "Thomas Hobbes" in Leo Straus and Joseph Cropsey (eds.), *History of Political Philosophy.* Third Edition. Chicago: University of Chicago Press. p.402. Also see Hobbes, Thomas (1968). *Leviathan*, edited by C.B. MacPherson. New York: Penguin Books.

14. Smith, Adam (1937). *An Inquiry into the Nature and Causes of the Wealth of Nations.* New York: Random House. Book V, Chapter 1, p.653.

15. Kant, Immanuel (1991). "Idea for a Universal History with a Cosmopolitan Purpose", reprinted in Hans Reiss (ed.), *Kant: Political Writings.* New York: Cambridge University Press p.47.

16. Ibid.: 45–6.

must be, in practice, a bad government."[18] Although James Madison's contributions to the *Federalist Papers* focused more on constraining than bolstering governmental power, he echoed Hamilton's view that government was needed as "a bulwark against foreign danger" and a "conservator of peace among ourselves."[19] Consequently, governance and control decrease the probability of an insurgency. They signal credibility and facilitate direct monitoring and control of the population.[20] Law and order within a state, then, depend on the government's ability to provide it.

So how does weak governance contribute to the outbreak of an insurgency? The logic is straightforward. Insurgencies are likely to develop and acquire civilian support where state control has declined or collapsed. By definition, weak states cannot meet the basic needs of their population.[21] They cannot consolidate authority over all their territory and they often do not succeed in maintaining order within the territory they do control.[22] They fail to use state resources to support security and policing activities that serve the public interest or to carry on routine administration.[23] Weak states lack Max Weber's core identifying characteristic of an effective state: the ability to establish monopoly of the legitimate use of physical force within a given territory.[24] Civil society is weak and poorly organised, security forces serve the regime rather than state interests, and courts are corrupt, politicised, and ineffective. It is not just that law and political

17. Hamilton, Alexander, James Madison and John Jay (1992). *The Federalist* 9: 36-8. London: J.M. Dent.

18. Hamilton, Alexander, James Madison and John Jay (1992). *The Federalist* 70: 360. London: J.M. Dent.

19. Hamilton, Alexander, James Madison and John Jay (1992). *The Federalist* 14: 62. London: J.M. Dent.

20. Kalyvas. *The Logic of Violence in Civil War.* pp.124–32.

21. Stromseth, Wippman and Brooks. *Can Might Make Rights?* pp.137–40.

22. Easterly, William R. (2001). *The Elusive Quest for Growth: Economists' Adventures and Misadventures in the Tropics.* Cambridge, MA: MIT Press; Klitgaard, Robert E. (1995). *Institutional Adjustment and Adjusting to Institutions.* Washington DC: The World Bank; Walle, Nicolas va de (2001). *African Economies and the Politics of Permanent Crisis, 1979–1999.* Cambridge: Cambridge University Press; Tendler, Judith (1997). *Good Government in the Tropics.* Baltimore, MD: Johns Hopkins University Press.

23. Ayoob, Mohammed (2001). "State Making, State Breaking, and State Failure", in Chester Crocker, Fen Osler Hampson and Pamela Aall (eds.), *Turbulent Peace: The Challenges of Managing International Conflict.* Washington DC: U.S. Institute of Peace Press. p.130.

24. Weber. "Politics as a Vocation", n.9.

institutions in these states are ineffective. It is that the faith in law and political institutions that underpins policing and order does not exist.[25] Weak states lack sufficient bureaucratic and institutional structures to ensure the functioning of government. They often lack trained civil servants and can barely operate school systems, courts, welfare systems, or other essentials for social functioning.[26]

Poor governance increases the likelihood of insurgency because the state's security forces are usually weak and lack popular legitimacy. These forces may be badly financed and equipped, organisationally inept, corrupt, politically divided, and poorly informed about events at the local level.[27] While military and paramilitary forces play a key role, the police are perhaps the most critical component of local forces. They are the primary arm of the government focused on internal security matters. Unlike the military, the police usually have a permanent presence in cities, towns, and villages; a better understanding of the threat environment in these areas; and better intelligence. This makes them a direct target of insurgent forces, who often try to kill or infiltrate them.[28] An effective police force is critical to establishing law and order because there are limits to the use of military force. The enemy frequently holds little territory and refuses to fight for the territory that it does hold. Government military forces may be able to penetrate and garrison an insurgent area and, if well sustained, may reduce guerrilla activity. But once the situation in an area becomes untenable for insurgents, they will simply transfer their activity to another area and the problem remains unresolved.[29] A viable indigenous police force with a permanent presence in urban and rural areas is a critical component of counter-insurgency.

When state institutions are weak, opportunistic elements in society are able to take advantage.[30] Since the state is incapable of controlling

---

25. Stromseth, Wippman and Brooks. *Can Might Make Rights?* pp.137–140; Fukuyama. *State-Building.* pp.92–118; Ayoob. "State Making, State Breaking, and State Failure", n.24.
26. Hironaka. *Neverending Wars*, pp.42–6.
27. Byman. "Friends Like These", pp.79–115; Byman. *Going to War with the Allies You Have.*
28. Trinquier. *Modern Warfare*, p.43; Galula. *Counterinsurgency Warfare*, p.31.
29. As David Galula argues: "[C]onventional operations by themselves have at best no more effect than a fly swatter. Some guerrillas are bound to be caught, but new recruits will replace them as fast as they are lost." Galula. *Counterinsurgency Warfare*, p.72.
30. World Bank (2000). *Reforming Public Institutions and Strengthening Governance.* Washington DC; Einhorn, Jessica (2001). "The World Bank's Mission Creep", *Foreign Affairs* 80(5): 22–35.

its own territory, this weakness creates opportunities for insurgent groups. This is especially true in remote areas of the country, where insurgent groups can establish rural strongholds.[31] The more extreme the decline or absence of authority in a region, the more the population becomes "virgin territory" for those would become an alternative government.[32] Insurgents set up new institutions and use violence against alleged spies, whose execution leads directly to the guerrillas' control of territory.[33] Warlords and political entrepreneurs often flourish and finance their private militias through criminal activity, including trafficking in arms and drugs. Simple banditry—fuelled by military desertion, the breakdown of social structures, and demobilisation of government forces—may be endemic. Ordinary crime can also escalate sharply because of a combination of economic necessity, social breakdown, the focus of forces on political and regime security, and proliferation of weapons.[34] In the absence of political institutions capable of processing societal demands and ensuring compliance with the rule of law, political mobilisation can lead to civil strife and insurgency.[35]

Corruption can be a particularly invidious challenge. It can undermine support for the government and increase support for insurgents. Corruption hampers economic growth, disproportionately burdens the poor, undermines the rule of law, and damages government legitimacy. It has a supply side (those who give bribes) and a demand side (public officials who take them).[36] At its core, corruption is the misuse of entrusted power for private gain. It can involve high-level officials with discretionary authority over government policies or lower-level officials who make decisions about enforcing (or not enforcing) regulations. Corruption also slows economic growth. It is often responsible for funnelling scarce public resources away from projects that benefit the society and toward projects that benefit

31. Hironaka. *Neverending Wars.* pp.42–6.

32. Kalyvas. *The Logic of Violence in Civil War.* p.216; Wickham-Crowley, Timothy P. (1992). *Guerrillas and Revolution in Latin America: A Comparative Study of Insurgents and Regimes since 1956.* Princeton, NJ: Princeton University Press. p.35.

33. Anderson, Jon Lee (2004). *Guerrilla: Journeys in the Insurgent World.* New York: Penguin. pp.212–13.

34. Stromseth, Wippman and Brooks. *Can Might Make Rights?.* pp. 17–40.

35. Paris. *At War's End.* pp.179–211.

36. Transparency International (2006). *Global Corruption Report 2006.* Berlin.

specific individuals. It hinders the development of markets and distorts competition, thereby deterring investment. However, the most damaging effect of corruption is its impact on the social fabric of society: corruption undermines the people's trust in the political system, political institutions, and political leadership.[37]

Historical Insights

The evidence from past insurgencies shows that weak and ineffective governance is critical to the onset of insurgencies. Statistical research suggests a strong correlation between weak governance and the germination of an insurgency. Political scientists David Laitin and James Fearon, who examined all civil wars and insurgencies between 1945 and 1999, found that "financially, organizationally, and politically weak central governments render insurgency more feasible and attractive due to weak local policing or inept and corrupt counterinsurgency practices."[38] In their study of 151 cases over a 54-year period, political scientists Michael Doyle and Nicholas Sambanis found that governance is critical to prevent and end civil wars and insurgencies. They argued that success requires the "provision of temporary security, the building of new institutions capable of resolving future conflicts peaceably, and an economy capable of offering civilian employment to former soldiers and material progress to future citizens."[39] Another study found that governmental capacity is a negative and significant predictor of civil war, and between 1816 and 1997 "effective bureaucratic and political systems reduced the rate of civil war activity."[40] Weak governance also contributes to lengthier insurgencies and civil wars. Insurgencies with outside support are on average 300 per cent longer than wars without intervention.[41]

Case studies support the link between weak states and insurgencies. The legacy of colonisation contributed to weak governance, since most colonies of the post-World War II era were unprepared for independence

37. Kaufmann. "Myths and Realities of Governance and Corruption". pp.81–98.

38. Fearon and Laitin. "Ethnicity, Insurgency, and Civil War". pp.75–6.

39. Doyle, Michael W. and Nicholas Sambanis (2006). *Making War and Building Peace*. Princeton, NJ: Princeton University Press. p.5.

40. Hironaka. *Neverending Wars*. p.45.

41. Ibid.: 51.

when it arrived. The imperial powers put little thought or effort into building up domestic governance structures in their colonies that could function on their own.[42] A few colonies, such as India and Sri Lanka, had been allowed a degree of self-government. But others, such as Somaliland, were little more than outposts. Somalia struggled with a weak state after its independence in 1960, and experienced several major insurgencies. The structural fragmentation of the Somali state was a relic of the circumstances of its independence, which required the unification of two separate colonial administrative structures. Each half of Somalia had its own judicial system, currency, administrative rules, taxation rates, accounting systems, and legal histories, which had to be unified into a single system.[43] Somalia also faced the standard quandary of a lack of resources. As one scholar noted, Somalia confronted "a depressing future as a perpetually impoverished Third World country with very few natural resources, constantly burdened by drought and the refugees from Ethiopia."[44] Somalia's security forces also lacked the capacity to contain conflict. As one study concluded, the country reverted to its status in the 19th century with no internationally recognised polity; no national administration exercising real authority; no formal legal system; no banking and insurance system; no police and public security service; no electricity or piped water system; and weak officials serving on a voluntary basis surrounded by violent bands of armed youths.[45]

In the Philippines, the weak state under Ferdinand Marcos was a major factor that contributed to the insurgency that began in 1972. The army was "rotten to the core" and rampantly corrupt.[46] Marcos was also corrupt. He dismantled the democratic structures the US had bequeathed to the country and ran a venal government. His tenure

42. See, for example, Herbst, Jeffrey (1996/97). "Responding to State Failure in Africa", *International Security* 21(3): 120–44 (Winter).

43. Laitin, David D. and Said S. Samatar (1987). *Somalia: Nation in Search of a State*. Boulder, CO: Westview Press; Lewis, I.M. (1988). *A Modern History of Somalia: Nation and State in the Horn of Africa*. Boulder, CO: Westview Press; Doyle and Sambanis. *Making War and Building Peace*. pp.145–61.

44. Brogan, Patrick (1998). *World Conflicts*. Lanham, MD: Scarecrow Press. p.99.

45. Adam, Hussein M. (1995). "Somalia: A Terrible Beauty Being Born?", in I. William Zartman (ed.), *Collapsed States: The Disintegration and Restoration of Legitimate Authority*. Boulder, CO: Lynne Rienner. p.78.

46. Kessler, Richard J. (1989). *Rebellion and Repression in the Philippines*. New Haven, CT: Yale University Press. p.140.

reduced an already poor country to near insolvency.[47] In Lebanon, a delicate sectarian balance led to the emergence of a weak state in the 1970s and as a consequence, the inability to implement substantive administrative reforms. The prevailing political system tended to foster corruption and laxity in upholding the public interest. The weak state fuelled competition between the three leading religious communities—the Maronites, Sunnis, and Shi'a—and triggered an insurgency from 1975 to 1991.[48] A weak state in Mozambique led to infighting in various regions of the country in 1976 and the rise of an insurgency.[49] After the collapse of the Soviet Union, weak state institutions in Georgia played a major role in a series of insurgencies. As one study concluded: "The causes of the three Georgian wars shared some similarities. Institutional weakness was a shared element in all three."[50] In Bosnia, state failure as a result of the crumbling Communist Party apparatus gave way to war across the Balkans in the early 1990s. War in the Balkans was caused by "the collapse of central authority in Yugoslavia. The secession of Slovenia and Croatia led quickly to the disintegration of this weakly-held-together ethnofederal Republic, creating fears of ethnic dominance among Bosnia Serbs and Muslims and fuelling irredentist nationalism in Serbia."[51]

Many states are so weak that they cannot establish order in peripheral geographic areas. These gaps are filled by insurgents. In Cuba, Fidel Castro and his guerrillas used the Sierra Maestra mountains as a base of support to train new recruits, rearm and regroup, and prepare for forays into the countryside.[52] In Peru, Shining Path guerrillas were based in the region of Ayacucho, a rural area that had historically received little government attention and control. As the

47. Chapman, William (1987). *Inside the Philippine Revolution.* New York: W.W. Norton.

48. Makdisi, Samir and Richard Sadaka (2005). "The Lebanese Civil War, 1975–1990", in Paul Collier and Nicholas Sambanis. *Understanding Civil War.* Vol. 2. pp.59–85. Washington DC: The World Bank.

49. Weinstein, Jeremy M. and Laudemiro Francisco (2005). "The Civil War in Mozambique: The Balance Between Internal and External Influences", in Collier and Sambanis Ibid.: 57–92.

50. Zurcher, Christopher, Pavel Baev, and Jan Koehler (2005)."Civil Wars in the Caucasus". in Collier and Sambanis Ibid.: 273.

51. Doyle and Sambanis. *Making War and Building Peace,* pp. 162–3.

52. Clodfelter, Micheal (1992). *Warfare and Armed Conflicts: A Statistical Reference.* Jefferson, NC: McFarland.

editor of a Peruvian newspaper argued: "There has traditionally been no government presence in many areas [of Ayacucho]...Hence...there are no liberated areas, only abandoned areas."[53]

In Congo, the insurgency that began in 1960 in the Katanga Province was based on fundamental structural weaknesses inherited from Congo's colonial legacy. To the degree that any state structure existed, it was "virtually improvis[ed] from scratch", and was essentially a replica of the Belgian constitution that had been revised for the Congo only five months ago.[54] The constitutional framework of the government collapsed less than three months after independence. As one study concluded about Congo: "These structural weaknesses, plus the lack of governmental capacity, the lack of geographic cohesion, and the lack of an established political system, made fragmentation in the form of secessionist attempts likely."[55] When Angola became independent in 1975, it inherited a weak state structure. The state suffered from a lack of adequate governmental capacity, bureaucratic structures, and governmental experience. Nearly all of the skilled labour in the country was Portuguese, and 90 per cent of the Portuguese fled the country leading up to Independence. This loss of skilled labour led to plummeting agricultural exports and the collapse of the service sector.[56] These structural weaknesses directly contributed to the rise of an insurgency.

In areas where governance is weak, insurgents seek to secure power at the local level, even if they cannot hope to seize the state at the national level. This means conquering and keeping territory to the extent possible.[57] Insurgents engage in state-like activities: they collect taxes, organise policing, administer justice, and conscript fighters. In

---

53. Marks, Thomas A. (1996). *Maoist Insurgency since Vietnam*. Portland, OR: Frank Cass. p.261.
54. Young, Crawford (1965). *Politics in the Congo: Decolonization and Independence*. Princeton, NJ: Princeton University Press. p.56.
55. Hironaka. *Neverending Wars*. p.94.
56. Minter, William (1994). *Apartheid's Contras*. Atlantic Highlinds, NJ: Zed Books; Fituni, Leonid L. (1995). "The Collapse of the Socialist State: Angola and the Soviet Union", in I. William Zartman (ed.), *Collapsed States*. Boulder, CO: Lynne Rienner. pp.143–56.
57. Wood, Elisabeth Jean (2003). *Insurgent Collective Action and Civil War in El Salvador*. Cambridge: Cambridge University Press. p.135; Romero, Mauricio (2000). "Changing Identities and Contested Settings: Regional Elites and the Paramilitaries in Colombia", *International Journal of Politics, Culture, and Society* 14(1): 51–69; Schofield, Victoria (1984). *Every Rock, Every Hill: The Plain Tale of the North-West Frontier and Afghanistan*. London: Buchan and Enright. p.308.

short, they enjoy a local monopoly on violence, which they use to punish their enemies and sanction non-compliance.

In the Canipaco Valley of Central Peru, according to one study,

> Shining Path assumed control and organized every aspect of the inhabitants' daily life. Sendero undertook the administration of justice and played the role of a moralising force. Shining Path settled marital conflicts, supervised the work of teachers, mediated the relationships between the communeros and those authorities and state functionaries who were not obliged to quite, executed thieves who robbed livestock from the herders and even organised recreation.[58]

In Vietnam, the Vietcong were able to establish a highly sophisticated five-level "shadow" administrative infrastructure run by close to 40,000 full-time employees by the end of 1968. As one study concluded, "one of the striking conclusions from interviewing [Vietcong] defectors is the total absence of the government movement in revolutionary areas for years at a time, except an occasional large-scale sweep operations which had little impact on the Party's local apparatus."[59] According to another account, "peasants conscripted into the revolutionary organisation became more than soldiers in a temporary fighting force; they potentially became subjects integrated into a new institution founding the basis for a nation-state."[60] In the early 1950s in the Philippines during the Huk insurgency, "one government was legal, but in these areas had little or no physical control. The insurgent government was illegal, but had partial or complete control and enforcement capability."[61]

The reverse is also true: strong governance can prevent insurgencies. Che Guevara brought disaster to his followers in Bolivia partly because he insisted on basing his campaign there on a cause (revolution throughout South America) that did not enjoy popular support in Bolivia, which had a relatively strong state.[62] There was a strong possibility of an insurgency in Kenya in the 1980s because of intense ethnic antagonisms, electoral violence, and a coup attempt in

58. Manrique, Nelson (1998). "The War for the Central Sierra", in Steve J. Stern (ed.), *Shining and Other Paths: War and Society in Peru, 1980–1995*. Durham, NC: Duke University Press. p.204.

59. Race, Jeffrey (1973). *War Comes to Long An: Revolutionary Conflict in a Vietnamese Province*. Berkeley: University of California Press. p.199.

60. Berman, Richard (1974). *Revolutionary Organization: Institution-Building within the People's Liberation Armed Forces*. Lexington, MA: D.C. Heath. pp.4–5.

61. Jones, Adrian H. and Andrew R. Molnar (1966). *Internal Defense against Insurgency: Six Cases*. Washington DC: Center for Research in Social Systems. p.47.

62. Galula. *Counterinsurgency Warfare*. p.29.

August 1982. But the relative strength of the state helped avert major violence.[63] Despite deep concerns about insurgencies in such countries as Kazakhstan and Uzbekistan, there were none. One major factor was the rise of strong, though undemocratic, governments that were able to control their minority (and majority) populations. Large-scale insurgencies are extremely rare events. As one study concludes, "the mean figure of actual violent communal events as a percentage of potential events hovers around zero."[64]

Afghanistan's Governance Woes

What explains the rise of Afghanistan's insurgency? "The answer is simple", one senior Afghan government official told me in October 2007. "The people are losing faith in the government. Our security forces cannot protect local villages, and our institutions struggle to deliver basic services."

At its core, the insurgency in Afghanistan is not about religion, as some mistakenly believe. Most Afghans in rural villages do not subscribe to the extremist views of the Taliban, al-Qaeda, or other insurgent groups such as Hizb-i-Islami—though they have tried to exploit religion. Most locals don't want to establish a radical and rather unorthodox interpretation of Islam, typified by one Taliban sign posted when they conquered Kabul in 1996: "Throw reason to the dogs. It stinks of corruption."[65] Indeed, most opinion polls suggested that the Taliban were not well liked in Afghanistan. A poll commissioned by the US Central Command in 2007, for example, indicated that 15 per cent of Afghans favour a Taliban return. In general, the problem was not that most Afghans inherently supported the Taliban. It was that patience with the Afghan government was breaking down.

As with most insurgencies, the critical precondition in Afghanistan was the collapse of governance. The Afghan government faced challenges providing basic services to the population; its security

63. Kimenyi, Mwangi S. and Njuguna S. Ndung'u (2005). "Sporadic Ethnic Violence: Why Has Kenya Not Experienced a Full-Blown Civil War?", in Paul Collier and Nicholas Sambanis (eds.), *Understanding Civil War, Vol. 1: Africa*. Washington DC: The World Bank. pp.123–56.

64. Laitin, David D. and James Fearon (1996). "Explaining Interethnic Cooperation", *American Political Science Review* 90(4): 717 (December).

65. Burke, Jason (2003). *Al-Qaeda: Casting a Shadow of Terror*. London: I.B. Tauris. p.111.

forces, especially police, had difficulty establishing law and order; and too few international forces filled the gap.

The new Afghan government had difficulty providing essential services to the population, especially in rural areas of the country. As one World Bank study concluded, the primary beneficiaries of assistance were the urban elite.[66] This triggered deep-seated frustration and resentment among the rural population. Indeed, the Afghan government suffered from a number of systemic problems, and had difficulty attracting and retaining skilled professionals with management and administrative experience. Weak administration and lack of control in some provinces made tax policy and administration virtually impossible. In many rural areas, the government made no effort to collect taxes. Electricity is a good example. In 2005, only 6 per cent of the Afghan population had access to power from the electricity grid.[67] And most of it was characterised by low voltage, intermittent supply, and blackouts. The dire situation reflected a lack of investment by the government and international community, as well as poor maintenance.

In addition to insufficient generation capacity (which was augmented by imports of power from neighbouring countries), the system was plagued by inadequate transmission, poor distribution, and lack of back-up equipment. Most efforts focused on supplying electricity in urban areas of the country, not on targeting rural areas in danger of falling to the Taliban. The government's electricity strategy was to "increase coverage of the electricity grid in urban areas to 90 per cent by 2015."[68] For those rich enough to buy generators, electricity was not a problem. The striking feature of Afghanistan's economic structure was the dominance of the informal sector. A large portion of the electricity supply, for example, was provided by small-scale generators.[69] The result was significant. As one World Bank assessment noted,

> The bulk of Afghans still do not have reliable electric power supply and clean water. Thus the situation that prevailed in the 1970s and during the long

---

66. World Bank (2005). *Afghanistan: State Building, Sustaining Growth, and Reducing Poverty.* Washington DC. p.xxvi.

67. Ibid.: 83.

68. Ibid.: 86.

69. World Bank (2004). *Afghanistan: State Building, Sustaining Growth, and Reducing Poverty.* Report No. 29551-AF. Washington DC. pp.5, 16.

period of conflict—basic social services not reaching most of Afghanistan's people—has not yet been fundamentally changed with the partial exception of primary education.[70]

In addition, the Afghan government faced challenges providing security outside of the capital. A major reason was the poor state of the Afghan National Police. The result was a weak security apparatus that could not establish monopoly of the legitimate use of force within the country. The police were not an international priority after the overthrow of the Taliban regime, and they received significantly less money and attention than the army. The United States declined to provide significant assistance to the Afghan police in the aftermath of the Taliban's overthrow, and handed police training over to the Germans. By 2003, however, the US officials at the State Department, Defense Department, and White House began to argue that the German effort was far too slow, trained too few police officers, and was seriously under-funded. Consequently, the State Department's Bureau of International Narcotics and Law Enforcement contracted DynCorp International to train the police. But by 2004, officials in the White House and the Department of Defense expressed concern that the State Department's effort was failing. Secretary of Defense Donald Rumsfeld wrote a series of "snowflakes" expressing concern that the police programme was undermining the US and broader NATO counter-insurgency efforts.[71] Key problems included the failure to conduct follow-on mentoring of Afghan police, to provide significant institutional reform in the Ministry of Interior, and to curb deep-seated corruption in the police and Ministry of Interior. In 2005, the US military took the lead in providing training, equipment, and other assistance to the Afghan National Police.

Nevertheless, the competence of the Afghan police remained low. As a German assessment of the border police noted, "Neither the Afghan border police nor the customs authorities are currently in a position to meet the challenges presented by this long border."[72] Internal US government documents expressed deepening alarm at the state of the Afghan police. A report by the Offices of Inspector General of the US

70. Ibid.: 99.

71. Secretary Rumsfeld's "snowflakes" were internal memos to his staff; he sometimes produced as many as sixty of them per day.

72. Government of Germany (2006). *Assessment of Doha II Conference on Border Management in Afghanistan: A Regional Approach*. Berlin: Government of Germany. p.2.

Departments of State and Defense concluded that the Afghan police's "readiness level to carry out its internal security and conventional police responsibilities is far from adequate. The obstacles to establish a fully professional [Afghan National Police] are formidable." It found that key obstacles included "no effective field training officer (FTO) program, illiterate recruits, a history of low pay and pervasive corruption, and an insecure environment."[73] The Afghan police were needed to help establish order in urban and rural areas. But they were heavily outgunned by insurgent forces, plagued by corruption, and lacked any semblance of a national police infrastructure. They lacked uniforms, armoured vehicles, weapons, ammunition, police stations, police jails, national command and control, and investigative training.[74] An Afghan trucker put it succinctly: "Forget about the Taliban, our biggest problems are with the police."[75]

An assessment by Afghanistan's intelligence service, the National Directorate for Security, concluded that there were too few competent Afghan forces to provide security to the people in the rural areas. "When villagers and rural communities seek protection from the police", it concluded, "either it arrives late or arrives in a wrong way." The government's security forces did not enjoy monopoly of power. Villagers who collaborated with the government or openly supported it often put themselves in grave danger. They were threatened or killed, and their bodies were hung in the centre of the village. This message was clear and effective. Those who wished to collaborate with the government or NATO forces had to stop, or move their families to the cities in search of protection. The result was that key villages fell into the hands of the Taliban and other insurgent groups. The villages were gradually emptied of pro-government political forces and individuals. These rural areas became sanctuaries for the Taliban and the people were left with no choice but to become sympathisers of the insurgents.

---

73. Inspectors General, US Department of State and US Department of Defense (2006). *Interagency Assessment of Afghanistan Police Training and Readiness*. Washington DC. p.1.
74. General Barry R. McCaffrey (ret.) (2006). Memorandum of Trip to Afghanistan and Pakistan to Colonel Mike Meese and Colonel Cindy Jebb, United States Military Academy, June; General Barry R. McCaffrey (ret.) (2007). Memorandum of Trip to Afghanistan and Pakistan to Colonel Mike Meese and Colonel Cindy Jebb, United States Military Academy, February.
75. Quoted in Sands, Chris (2007). "Bring Back Taliban to End Police Corruption, Say Afghan Truckers", *The Independent* (London), 10 May.

Outside Support

Afghanistan also faced challenges from outside actors, which undermined governance. The first was a limited NATO role. Its roots hearkened back to the "light footprint" approach adopted by the United States and other international actors—including the United Nations—in 2001. Senior policymakers wanted to avoid a heavy footprint like the Soviet Union had used in Afghanistan which, they argued, triggered the anti-Soviet insurgency in the 1980s. In addition, the US war in Iraq shifted attention and resources from Afghanistan as early as November 2001, when planning efforts for Iraq began. The result in Afghanistan has been a light footprint ever since.

In 2007, for example, ISAF was still 3000 troops short of its manpower goal in the south, and its ability to sustain current force levels and capabilities over the longer term was tenuous. As NATO General David Richards argued in testimony before the British House of Commons, the level of troop numbers was his most significant concern:

> Simply being able to move their troops from the North to the South would not have been a solution to me at all because we have got just about the right number of troops in the North to contain the situation there, which is broadly stable...What I was really after was...an increase in the overall number of troops.[76]

These numbers were particularly insufficient because a number of NATO countries refused to become involved in combat operations.

This practice was referred to as "national caveats", and was triggered by several concerns. A number of NATO countries had a different philosophy about how to operate in Afghanistan and how to conduct counter-insurgency operations. They were particularly adamant that stabilisation and reconstruction efforts were the recipe for success in Afghanistan. Combat operations were likely to alienate the population, especially if they led to civilian casualties. As a British House of Commons investigation concluded: "In Madrid, we were told by politicians and academics that while Spanish public opinion supported troops working on reconstruction projects in Afghanistan, it would not support a war-fighting role. In Berlin, we were told about the constitutional restrictions on Germany's military operating abroad."[77]

---

76. UK House of Commons Select Committee on Defence (2007). *Thirteenth Report*. London: HMSC. para. 46.

77. Ibid., para. 43.

In addition, political leaders were reluctant to deploy their forces into violent areas because of low domestic support for combat operations. In a German Marshall Foundation poll, for example, 75 per cent of Germans, 70 per cent of Italians, and 72 per cent of Spaniards did not support the deployment of their troops for combat operations in Afghanistan.[78]

Second, most major insurgent groups—including the Taliban—had sanctuary in Pakistan. Several of the Taliban's key leaders were based in the vicinity of Quetta, Pakistan. The Taliban had a series of financial propaganda, and other committees in such areas as Karachi and Peshawar. Elements of Pakistan's government—including its Frontier Corps and the ISI—were also involved in assisting the Taliban and other groups. And the Afghanistan-Pakistan border was a sieve for arms, suicide bombers, fighters, improvised explosive devices, and other logistical support to insurgent groups.

Addressing Key Challenges

There are no short-term solutions for defeating insurgent groups, and it has taken an average of 14 years for governments to defeat insurgent groups. Many also end in a draw, with neither side winning. Insurgencies can also have long tails: approximately 25 per cent of insurgencies won by the government and 11 per cent won by insurgents last more than 20 years.[79] If one starts counting in 2002, when the Taliban began conducting limited offensive operations, history suggests that it would take on average until 2016 to win.

This does not mean, however, that NATO countries need to—or should—win the insurgency for the Afghans. Quite the reverse. While outside actors often play an important role, victory is usually a function of the struggle between the local government and insurgents. First, outside forces are unlikely to remain for the duration of any counter-insurgency effort, at least as a major combatant force. Since indigenous forces eventually have to win the war on their own, they must develop the capacity to do so. If they don't develop this capacity,

---

78. German Marshall Fund of the United States and the Compagnia di San Paolo (Italy) (2007). *Transatlantic Trends: Key Findings 2007.* Washington DC. p.33.

79. Jones, Seth G. (2008). *Counterinsurgency in Afghanistan.* Santa Monica, CA: RAND.

indigenous forces are likely to lose the war once international assistance ends. Second, indigenous forces usually know the population and terrain better than external actors and are better able to gather intelligence. Third, a lead outside role may be interpreted by the people as an occupation, eliciting nationalist reactions that impede success. Fourth, a lead indigenous role can provide a focus for national aspirations and show the people that they—and not foreign forces—control their own destiny. This means that NATO countries can be helpful in assisting the Afghan government. Three steps may be helpful.

Improving Governance

The first is arresting and prosecuting key individuals involved in corruption and criminal activity, including Afghan government officials. The root cause of most insurgencies has been the collapse of governance. One helpful step in Afghanistan would be directly dealing with corruption in the Afghan government, which contributed to a decline of support. As Figure 4.1 highlights, an Asia Foundation poll found that a striking 77 per cent of respondents said corruption was a major problem in Afghanistan; 66 per cent believed corruption was a major problem in the provincial government; 42 per cent said corruption was a major problem in their daily life; and 40 per cent said corruption was a major problem in their neighbourhood. Moreover, most Afghans believed that the corruption problem was getting worse. Approximately 60 per cent of the respondents believed that corruption had increased over the past year at the national level, and 50 per cent believed that it had increased at the provincial level. Many had been directly involved in bribery, such as providing cash to a government official. Indeed, 36 per cent said they had been involved in bribery with a police officer, 35 per cent with a court official, and 34 per cent with officials in applying for work.[80] Those in southern and western Afghanistan were most likely to say they had personally experienced corruption; those in central and northern Afghanistan were the least likely.[81]

---

80. Asia Foundation (2006). *Afghanistan in 2006: A Survey of the Afghan People.* Kabul: The Asia Foundation. pp.14–16.

81. Weber, Stephen *et al.* (2006). *Afghan Public Opinion Amidst Rising Violence.* College Park, MD: Program on International Policy Attitudes, University of Maryland. December. p.6.

Corrupt government officials, including those involved in the drug trade, should be removed from office. There is no shortage of intelligence on who they are. The most effective way to do this may be to begin with the "lowing hanging fruit": capturing and prosecuting individuals where there is solid evidence of criminal behaviour.

Figure 4.1

Prevalence of Corruption

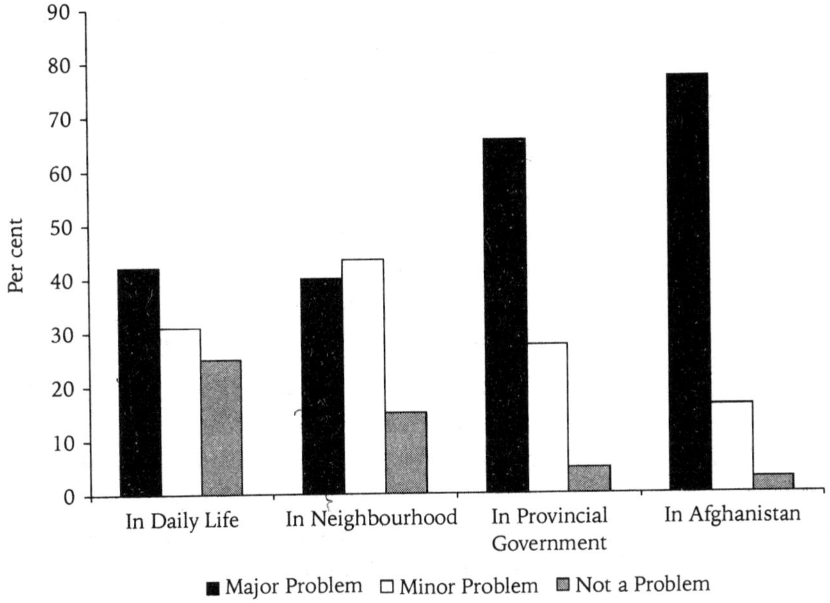

Source: Asia Foundation (2006). *Afghanistan in 2006*, p.14.

Shifting the Centre of Gravity

The second step is increasing NATO and Afghan National Army resources in the south. The Taliban's heartland has traditionally been in the south, including in such provinces as Kandahar. This is where the focus of NATO's counter-insurgency efforts should be, and this is where NATO is most in danger of losing. The south represents the insurgents' centre of gravity. British and Canadian efforts have been Herculean; but they need help in clearing and holding territory. Bringing in NATO countries with limited or no experience operating in the midst of a violent insurgency would be counterproductive. A better option would be deploying a sufficient number of forces—at a bare minimum 3000—from such nations as the United States, who can more effectively conduct counter-insurgency operations. Also necessary are increased efforts to build competent Afghan national security forces. Deploying a greater number of Afghan National Army soldiers who can help clear and hold territory would be ideal in the south. The Afghan National Police are in poor shape. Most are under-trained, poorly equipped, corrupt, and not always loyal to the government. One of the most significant challenges with the police is in mentoring, including in the south. They need help from mentors in the field—at checkpoints, on patrols, and at police stations.

Dealing with Neighbours

The third step is conducting sustained operations against the Taliban, al-Qaeda, and other militant groups in Pakistan. An effective strategy is badly needed to undermine insurgent groups operating out of Pakistan's border regions. In past insurgencies, the ability of insurgent groups to gain external sanctuary and support from outside actors has significantly increased their probability of winning.

One key area is addressing tensions between India and Pakistan, which are a root cause of the problem. Pakistan and India have long been involved in a balance-of-power struggle in South Asia. Both lay claim to the Kashmir region, and have fought several wars over Kashmir since 1947. Since 2001, India has become Afghanistan's closest strategic partner in the region. India has provided more than $1 billion in financial assistance to Afghanistan since 2001. It has funded a variety of reconstruction projects, including the new Afghan parliament building, and provided assistance to Afghan legislators. India has also established a number of consulates near the Afghan-Pakistani border. Pakistan has accused these consulates of collecting intelligence and helping foment unrest in the Pakistani province of Balochistan. The Indian-Afghan alliance has left Pakistan deeply insecure. Some Pakistan officials argue that India has surrounded Pakistan on its main eastern and western flanks, which include 80 per cent of its borders. This encirclement has caused the Pakistan government to support proxy groups operating out of the tribal areas and Kashmir. Ameliorating Pakistan's security concerns is vital. As long as Pakistan sees India as a threat on its eastern and western flanks, it will have significant incentives to establish proxy groups operating in the tribal areas and Balochistan province.

The development gap in Pakistan's Pashtun areas needs to be addressed. It is also a root cause of extremism. Government institutions in the tribal areas are weak, and social and economic conditions are among the lowest in the world. Currently, international reconstruction and development assistance has focused on the Afghan side of the border. But this strategy is a half-measure. International assistance needs to be directed toward Pakistan's tribal areas, not just Afghanistan.

As part of this broader development strategy, NATO could also encourage Afghanistan and Pakistan to settle their border disagreement, siding with Pakistan. These negotiations should probably begin in earnest after the next Afghan presidential elections in 2009, since they will be divisive. No government of Afghanistan has ever formally recognised the British-drawn Durand Line, established in 1893, that divides control over Pashtun territories between Afghanistan and what was then British India. The Durand Line continues to be a source of tension between Afghanistan and Pakistan. The negotiations should ultimately aim to establish an outcome in which Afghanistan agrees to the current internationally recognised border, the tribal territories of Pakistan are integrated into and receive a full range of services from Pakistan, and the border area becomes a region for cooperative development rather than insecurity.

Pakistan needs to conduct a sustained campaign against key Taliban, al-Qaeda, and other extremist forces residing in Pakistan. This should be primarily a law enforcement and intelligence operation, not a military one. Sustained Pakistani military operations in the tribal areas would be too destabilising, especially since the tribes often regard outside forces—including the Pakistani military—as unwelcome foreigners. Pushing President Musharraf to conduct a sustained campaign against insurgents will also require finding pressure points that raise the costs of stalling. Perhaps the most significant is tying current American assistance to cooperation. The United States gives Pakistan over $1 billion in military and economic assistance each year. This assistance covers such areas as health, economic development, trade, and law enforcement. The United

States could tie assistance in some of these areas—as well as implicit American support in multilateral bodies such as the World Bank and the International Monetary Fund—to progress in defeating Afghan insurgents and their support network.

Moving Forward

David Galula, a French military officer, argued that the "best cause for the insurgent's purpose is one that, by definition, can attract the largest number of supporters and repel the minimum of opponents."[82] In Afghanistan, there was a supply of disgruntled villagers unhappy with their government, and a demand for recruits by ideologically motivated leaders. Too little outside support for the government and too much support for insurgents further undermined governance. This combination proved deadly for the onset—and continuation—of the insurgency.

Afghanistan is not hopeless. According to the World Bank, for example, Afghanistan's economy grew by an estimated 14 per cent in 2005 and 5.3 per cent in 2006.[83] Annual end-period inflation, as measured by the consumer price index for Kabul, subsided to 4.8 per cent in 2007. Annual end-period "national" inflation, covering Kabul and five other cities, was 3.9 per cent in 2007.[84] Democracy returned after a 30-year hiatus, hearkening back to Zahir Shah's "blueprint for democracy" period in the 1960s and early 1970s. President Hamid Karzai has retained relatively high levels of support. According to a December 2007 public opinion poll, for instance, 63 per cent of Afghans rated the work of President Karzai positively.[85] This was a greater level of support than many Western leaders enjoy. In addition, several Afghan cities experienced a fundamental transition over the past few years. Kabul, for example, was awash in electronic equipment and a sprinkle of new Internet cafes. The streets were clogged with bright yellow taxicabs, watermelon carts, bicycles, and cars imported from Europe and Asia. Boys and girls shuffled to school along the city's congested sidewalks.

82. Galula. *Counterinsurgency Warfare*. pp.19–20.

83. World Bank (2007). *Afghanistan At a Glance*. Washington DC. p.1.

84. International Monetary Fund (2007). *Islamic Republic of Afghanistan: Second Review Under the Three-Year Arrangement under the Poverty Reduction and Growth Facility—Staff Report*. Washington DC. July. p.26.

85. ABC News/BBC/ARD (2007). *Afghanistan—Where Things Stand*. Kabul. 2007. p.16.

Construction projects dotted the city, including several new banks and a modern indoor shopping mall in Kabul City Centre. The city had been reduced to rubble a decade earlier.

But the Taliban and other groups engineered a competent insurgency from bases in Pakistan and Afghanistan. The insurgency will ultimately be won or lost in the rural areas of Afghanistan, not in the cities. Success in ending the insurgency will take time and sufficient resources. For a growing number of Afghans, history is repeating itself. The challenge for the Afghan government and its NATO allies is not an easy one. It involves providing security to the villages, especially in strategically important areas of the south and east. It also includes beginning to get a handle on the corruption that is gnawing away at the government and its fragile support base. Most Afghans are not asking for much. They want security and hope, and perhaps something to make their difficult lives a little better. After 30 years of near-constant war, they certainly deserve it.

5

The Future of Afghanistan

Appraising Alternatives

RASUL BAKHSH RAIS

Introduction

The three cycles of wars that Afghanistan has experienced over the past 30 years wiped out its accumulated institutional and political heritage, disrupting its natural evolution as a historical entity. Among other motives and interests, the Afghan groups and foreign actors involved in the conflict wanted to define and shape the future of the country according to their own respective power, security, and strategic interests. The extended wars suggest how important, difficult and complex reordering a state and society is, once its historical flow and social capacities to balance competing interests are lost. The quest for reordering Afghanistan has involved two interventions by the two superpowers of modern times and several bouts of internal struggles and civil wars amongst various Afghan factions. Why has the character of state been so contentious and why will it remain troublesome for the present and future coalitions? Why has it been so difficult to evolve consensus among the Afghans about what kind of state they would like Afghanistan to be? Why have foreign powers been so interested in determining the future of this historically isolated country? What type of state and nation is Afghanistan likely to be in the coming decades?

The present efforts, under a very broad international coalition of forces which aims to establish peace and reconstruct the country, represent a deep interest and a desire to transform Afghanistan from a failed state to a normal, governable, and effective state. This endeavour should not be dismissed as expedient, temporary or shaped by the merely negative motive of punishing a regime that hosted America's worst enemies. It is a serious nation-building project, which might have faults, but undoubtedly it has a clear vision—to pull Afghanistan out of chaos produced by the absence of state and by internecine internal conflicts.

Before we discuss what is really at stake for the Afghans, the regional states and the international community at large, it would be necessary to contextualise the ongoing nation-building project in Afghanistan within its history and geography. In doing so, let us make two raw propositions that rest on these factors which, in our view, have consistently impinged upon Afghanistan's struggle for modern statehood:

a Afghanistan's process of establishing a modern state started late, with a meagre institutional endowment and a convenient "rentier" mindset.

b The "frontier" character of the state constrained what the Afghan nation-builders aspired for and narrowed the scope of what realistically could be achieved.

These two characteristics might have overlapping effects on the quality of Afghanistan's statehood, in different ways and in varying degrees. Let us briefly touch on the first proposition. There is now a good amount of literature on why the state was not able to adequately strike roots deep in Afghan society and why its institutional reach was confined to a few areas of the country. One of the most impressive explanations of institutional deficit of the Afghan state is by Barnet Rubin. Professor Rubin finds the shallow roots in the habit of the Afghan elites and ruling oligarchy to seek support from outside to carry out primary functions of the state, including social and economic development.[1] For lack of vision and political capacity they avoided difficult decisions like extracting revenues from society, framing appropriate development strategies, and building political trust between the state and the society.

A rentier state's difficulty lies in its failure to assume corresponding obligations toward society when it takes something

1. Rubin, Barnett R. (1992). "Political Elite in Afghanistan: Rentier State Building, Rentier State Wrecking", *International Journal of Middle East Studies* 24: 78.

from it. These obligations are accountability, responsiveness, and transparency in the allocation of public funds. A state not depending on society and instead acquiring economic and political energies from outside sources has a tendency to become "autonomous", less obliged by and independent of society.[2] By being autonomous, it excludes society from collectively making political choices. By the logic of its separate but parallel existence, the state and society fail to develop the mutual bond that defines modern nation-states.

Unlike other rentier states, Afghanistan failed to sustain itself, let alone grow out of dependence. This failure occurred at a critical juncture when the Afghan state was evolving from an ancient kingdom to a nation-state in a post-colonial global power structure in the late 1960s. By then, it had embarked steadily on a course of institutional development in different areas of national life, which was greatly aided by the heritage of earlier modernisation efforts and the fresh attempts towards development undertaken by its monarchy and relatively small modernist elite present in the state institutions.[3]

Politically, Afghanistan was relatively more open with the introduction of the 1964 constitution and two elections. Parallel to this, debate and discussion in the educational institutions, local media, and multiple informal political organisations demonstrated a great departure from the old political climate of fear and restraint. There was latent political energy and eagerness among the new classes emerging out of the modern educational institutions and within the intellectual circles, to influence the direction of political change in the country. But they were not on one page about what identity, ideology, and developmental path Afghanistan would take. Greatly influenced by similar political ideas and movements within the region and beyond, the Afghans became divided into three ideological camps, which can be loosely defined as traditionalist, Islamists, modernists and socialists.

Although the modernists and the socialists diverged in their vision of Afghanistan, they shared a common threat in the rise of Islamist ideology and its growing popularity among students and the traditional class of *mullahs* (clergy), which was reflected in their greater

2. Ibid.
3. Saikal, Amin (2004). *Modern Afghanistan: A History of Struggle and Survival.* London: I.B. Tauris.

numbers in the 1969 elections. The coup of 1973 led by Sardar Mohammad Daoud presented the common anxieties and shared vision of nationalists, modernists, and socialists. The dream of transforming Afghanistan from a monarchy to a republic was short-lived. Internal rifts among the coalition partners, fatally incompatible outlooks, and growing militancy weakened Daoud and his hold on power. Finally, the socialist wing of the National Army encouraged and supported by their Soviet handlers captured power through a coup in April 1978.

The socialist revolution was the beginning of the end of the modern state that the Afghans wanted to construct. It was a very bold but unrealistic attempt to reorganise the state, society, and economy which the Afghans had known and lived through centuries. The coup-makers, in the conventional rhetoric of textbook revolutionaries saw every piece and aspect of Afghanistan as offensive, unwanted, rotten, and requiring a surgical change. This misreading of Afghanistan's history, society, and social relations made them foreigners in their own country. Their presence in the power structure, overtly propped up by the Soviet Union, was offensive to the Afghan sense of nationhood and nationalism, and consequently provoked a nationwide resistance against the socialists and their patron, the former Soviet Union.

There are many interpretations about the motives of internal and external actors who organised resistance against the socialists and the Soviet occupier, but there is general consensus that in the process of this conflict, hardly anyone emerged a victor.[4] In the conflict, one million lives were lost and about half of the population was dislocated internally or externally, millions of them forever. However, the greatest casualty of the war was the Afghan state; it was critically debilitated as the political and ideological fissures between the Afghan groups, which wanted to transform it according to their respective visions, further aggravated.

The story of Afghanistan's destruction cannot be complete or the tragedy of state destruction meaningfully analysed without understanding the "frontier" character of Afghanistan. It is the only state in the world, perhaps, which has majorities of the ethnic groups

4. Rais, Rasul Bakhsh (1990). *War Without Winners: Afghanistan's Uncertain Transition after the Cold War.* Karachi: Oxford University Press.

that make up Afghanistan in neighbouring states, retaining only a rump of them. In terms of ethnicity of its composite elements, Afghanistan is on the ethnic frontiers of regional states. The country was born out of dying empires in 1747, and what helped its birth was the frontier character of the Pashtun tribes as much as the geographic marginality of the new kingdom. As an accident of history it also found itself on the expanding frontiers of two European imperial powers, Russia and Britain, about a hundred years later. By then, the two imperial powers had firmly established themselves, one in the north and the other in the south of the country. Experiencing a severe deficiency of power, Afghanistan found itself in a geopolitical nutcracker, with hardly any room to move, manoeuvre, and shape its future independent of the wishes of the two great imperial powers.

Interestingly, Afghanistan was spared direct occupation by either, and the relatively more proactive and regionally stronger Britain succeeded in controlling its foreign affairs, relegating it to a glorious princely state on the patterns of hundreds of such states under the Raj in the subcontinent. Seen in the backdrop of the "great game", Russia and Britain did not want to share colonial borders, fearing that their mutual suspicions, fears, and anxieties might lead them to a costly conflict. With a clear motive they settled the Afghanistan issue by conceiving it as a "buffer" that would keep the two at some distance. However, Britain, not completely complaisant with this arrangement and relatively more fearful than Russia, kept a strong vigil over Afghanistan's internal situation, occasionally interfering to correct any deviation from the dotted lines. Hence, Afghanistan in more than one way was a "frontier" state, which negatively affected its institutional development and international status. Afghanistan's status as a frontier state also aided the continuation of the traditional domination of the Pashtun king and Pashtun-dominated oligarchy, which thwarted the country from achieving a semblance of internal consolidation amongst its various ethnic groups.

Afghanistan claimed its independence unilaterally in 1919, which was affirmed *de jure* through the Treaty of Rawalpindi in 1921. Afghanistan was free after 80 years and was able to independently shape its foreign and domestic policies under an enlightened *amir*, Amanullah Khan. His modernisation programme and social development agenda, inspired by the modernists in Iran and Turkey, failed to enthuse the traditional sectors of the society. Before his opponents got some steam and power to disrupt the implementation of his vision, he succeeded in sowing the seeds of modern Afghanistan in vital sectors, such as education, national army, documentation of economy, and development of modern bureaucracy. Modernisation under Amanullah Khan was the first decisive attempt to change Afghanistan's ancient regime—an attempt to build its future along modern lines.[5]

Afghanistan's problems did not end with successful reassertion of sovereignty over foreign affairs. The roots of many challenges it faced were mainly domestic. The state was confronted by dynastic rivalries, ethnic fragmentation, its own weak capacity to govern effectively, and expand its writ beyond the cities. Until the middle of the 20th century, Afghanistan remained a nominal state, leaving much of its population to the traditional structures of authority, local community leaders, tribal chiefs, and officialdom relatively subordinate to the locally influential figures in the vast rural periphery. The real move toward state-building started under King Zahir Shah with a great deal of assistance from varied international sources. This influenced the nature of the emerging state, its "rentier" and oligarchic disposition.

With new opportunities and international connectedness, Afghanistan's regional environment also changed significantly with the departure of the British from the subcontinent. It now faced an independent India—the land historically Afghanistan's national heroes and warriors had fancied and invaded with regular frequency for centuries. A greater change for Afghanistan was the emergence of the new state of Pakistan, which had the legacy of the Durand Line and a larger population of Pashtuns on its side compared to Afghanistan, the country that the Pashtuns founded and identified with. The regional changes, the Cold War power structure and the competitive globalism of the two superpowers greatly influenced Afghanistan's internal dynamics and shaped its foreign policy.

5. Poullada, Leon B. (1973). *King Amanullah's Failure to Modernize a Tribal Society.* Ithaca, NY: Cornell University Press; Khan, Abdul Rehman (1980). *The Life of Abdul Rahman: Amir of Afghanistan.* Karachi: Oxford University Press.

How did the new geopolitical configuration change Afghanistan's fundamental character as a "frontier" state? I would argue that it not only altered the fundamental character of the Afghan state, it also added complexity to its relationships with both its neighbouring states as well as the great powers. Afghanistan's location at the intersection of three strategic regions invoked the natural interest of all its neighbours concerning its state and nationhood, its political preferences, and the foreign policy choices it made. For this reason, some of the neighbouring states have been voluntarily or involuntarily involved in influencing the political direction of Afghanistan. This involvement has been both defensive—to prevent adversarial states taking control of the country—and offensive in order to keep other regional rivals out.

Far deadlier for Afghanistan was the ideological and strategic rivalry between the superpowers during the second wave of the Cold War that was significantly fuelled by the Soviet occupation of the country and national resistance against communism. Becoming a battleground of active hostility between the superpowers proved disastrous for the Afghan state and society. Afghanistan lost its traditional social balance, institutions and its ability to provide security, stability, and national cohesion.

As the complex conflict prolonged and social and state institutions of Afghanistan began to disintegrate, the power vacuum sucked in dangerous transnational militant groups with a globalist agenda. The use of Afghanistan as a sanctuary and as a base to operate from and strike at targets beyond Afghanistan has motivated distant powers to restructure Afghanistan's state and nationhood. Their military intervention and subsequent reconstruction efforts are premised on the belief that a stateless Afghanistan could pose a major threat to international stability and security. The Afghan groups, regional states and international players, all have a stake in the future of Afghanistan.

What future can we realistically speculate for Afghanistan in the coming years and decades? It is not even quite certain what kind of state and nation Afghanistan is likely to be. We may, however, speculate three alternative futures, which will have tremendous impact on the stability and security of the entire region. Three possible alternative futures are: effective statehood, fragmentation, and nominal state.

Effective Statehood

The present chapter of Afghanistan's political history started with the ouster of the Taliban by the international coalition of forces led by the United States and authorised by the United Nations. Removing a weak and vulnerable regime that ruled through fear and use of repression was perhaps the easiest part. However, faced with heavy bombardment on their fixed positions the battle-hardened Taliban commanders, with their tremendous experience of guerrilla warfare against the former Soviet Union, soon began to disperse among the local populations to prepare for the kind of war the Afghan terrain favours—insurgency.

Regime change in the country through use of force was presented to the Afghans as a way out of their internal feuds and troubles through the commitment of state and nation-building. Both the war and post-conflict reconstruction were conceived as a multinational and multi-institutional effort toward a common goal of securing and reviving the country. For more than six years, the international community has been involved in rebuilding Afghanistan as a normal and effective state. This is still a work in progress and continues to face many challenges.

This post-conflict reconstruction has borrowed heavily from the modernist theory and benefits from the hindsight of similar efforts elsewhere. However, post-conflict reconstruction is a difficult process for many reasons. Societies suffering from conflicts might have different social structures; the nature of internal combatants and their social support bases, regional environment, and responses of the neighbouring states and the effects on the state and society might vary. The policy instruments and the rebuilding packages may have significant common points but at the same time would have to address the uniqueness of each situation. Afghanistan is a distinct case of post-conflict reconstruction because of the three cycles of war that it experienced over three decades and the impact it left on social relations, ethnicity, and traditional institutions and authority structures.

There was hardly any remnant of political or state institution that could provide a base to rebuild the Afghan state. Reconstruction conveys the impression that old structures of power are being rebuilt or revived. But in Afghanistan it is a fresh and bold effort to build a new country without much borrowed from its past political experience.

The focal point of reconstructing Afghanistan is effective statehood—the political and institutional capacity to exercise sovereign writ and control all its territories, leaving no space ungoverned. This highly ambitious objective cannot be accomplished without adequate, sustained, and long-term international cooperation and assistance. The international community understood the enormity of the Afghan situation and the threat it posed if the country was left on its own. These reconstruction efforts of the international community are driven by its self-interest rather than altruism.

It appears that state- and nation-building in Afghanistan is an integrated, comprehensive, and holistic enterprise. It has involved all dimensions and aspects of the state from political, administrative, judicial institutions to provision of services and reconstruction of the economic infrastructure. Because of the nature of the destruction, political fragmentation, and multiple conflicts that left stubborn legacies, the larger questions of security and development had to be, and continue to remain two essential elements of the reconstruction strategy. The foremost issue was how to create a unified Afghan government representing all ethnic groups of the country that would assume control of the country in the wake of Taliban defeat or, what now appears to be, merely their retreat. It required a concerted international effort through the agency of the United Nations to invite the Afghan groups in a conference. Through a great deal of persuasion and diplomatic effort, the Afghans agreed to the Bonn process, which among other things established the interim government. The international backing and the consensus reached among the Afghan groups provided some semblance of legitimacy to the new power structure in Kabul.

Since then, Afghanistan has made significant progress in drafting a constitution, convening a *Loya Jirga* to ratify it, and holding presidential, parliamentary, and provincial elections.[6] In the backdrop of institutional and national power vacuum, these are no small achievements. Political reconstruction in post-conflict societies has been the key element in assisting the larger process of nation and state building. It is a key because every other aspect of state and society

6. Jalali, Ali A. (2006). "The Future of Afghanistan", *Parameters*: 4–17, Spring.

must grow out of the national consensus among the main societal components, elites, or key players, whatever name you prefer for them.

In the social and economic conditions of Afghanistan the very idea of a constitutional and representative government, no matter how flawed its procedural aspects, is transformative and revolutionary. It has provided Afghanistan a legal, normative base to build a new state for itself. There has been equally greater focus on building a judicial, legal system, training and reorganising bureaucracy, police and the national army. All state institutions with faded shades and traces of the old structures are still gradually evolving. Their capacity, growth, effectiveness, and success will eventually determine the effectiveness of the Afghan state.

Economic revival is another fundamental element of state building, having a considerable bearing on the state's stability, societal peace, and efficacy. But economic revival is not possible without rebuilding communications, roads, power generation, and agricultural infrastructure. Social services, such as education and health, are yet another important state functions, without which the desperate Afghan population, devastated by conflict and physical dislocation cannot be won over by the new state. The credit for progress or blame for failure of the Afghan state in all these areas will redound as much to the Afghan leaders as to the international community; the latter appears to have committed a lot but delivered very little in time and in places where the economic assistance was needed the most.

Overall, the achievements are mixed, and many aspects of reconstruction are in a transitional phase. There is a great deal of critique of the reconstruction priorities, failures in implementation of projects, corruption and mismanagement of resources.[7] The mist of pessimism about Afghanistan's future has not lifted as yet. In fact, the frequency of comments about its lapsing back to anarchy, disorder or civil war has increased during the past year.[8] There are old and new challenges that Afghanistan and the international community are genuinely interested in during its rehabilitation phase. These are: ethnic fragmentation, Taliban insurgency, drug economy, and warlordism. All

7. See Rubin, Barnett R. (2007). "Saving Afghanistan", *Foreign Affairs*, January/February.

8. Ibid.

these undermine reconstruction, and would benefit from its weakness or eclipse.

A Neutral State

Afghanistan's present and future stability is no less a function of its "frontier" character and the regional environment than the internal consensus or confrontation among its social groups. Its ethnic groups straddle the boundaries into other states where they form the majorities; Afghanistan contains remnant ethnic parts. Its majority Pashtun population, however, is larger than the Pashtun population in Pakistan. This ethnic distribution provokes fears, concerns and legitimate interest in the future of the country, and its politics and its security and foreign policy orientation. Historically, Afghanistan has been a buffer among contesting empires and a venue of separation and accommodation. Its post-colonial national assertion changed its self-definition without changing much of the regional realities that its neighbouring countries had inherited. One imprudent outcome of Afghanistan's national self-assertion was that it allowed the Soviet Union to penetrate its state institutions, in expectation that aligning with a superpower would provide it the means to develop as well as reassert its irredentist claims against Pakistan. Afghanistan's territorial ambitions were in sync with its historical and regional realities. Its gradual transformation from a buffer state into a strategic base of a superpower, however, proved extremely tragic.

In the post-Soviet civil war the regional states played a mini–Great Game, using different ethnic groups to advance their interests into the country. Afghanistan's warring factions provided the base for regional rivals to play out their political and strategic game. The Afghans would rephrase this, depending upon which Afghan group is talking.

In its new historical phase Afghanistan has to reassess what kind of state it is going to be. Success would depend on its self-perception, vision about the future, and ties with the regional states.

A Nominal or Failed State

Bleak scenarios about the future of Afghanistan are widely circulating. A belief is emerging that things in Afghanistan after seven years of security and economic assistance are not on the right track. Some analysts question the over-emphasis on combat operations that have taken attention and resources away from providing human security.[9] This comment does have merit; but in an insurgency-stricken province or region, what ought to come first—security or development—or should they run concurrently? There are no easy answers in the context of Afghanistan, particularly in the south and the east where the Taliban insurgency has been rising. The international coalition forces have tried to meet this challenge by putting together provincial reconstruction teams (PRTs) which, at best, have a mixed record of achievements.

The coalition forces differ greatly on the question of reconstruction priorities, use of force, commitment of troops, command structures, and other vital issues that would have a strong bearing on the outcome of the reconstruction process. The US would like member-states of the European Union to provide more troops and participate more in policing, drug interdiction, poppy eradication, and combat operations than they are apparently willing to offer.

The real challenge is the Taliban's growing power to destabilise the country. In the past two years they have emerged as a credible force with greater capacity to trouble the national army and foreign troops.[10] The Taliban finds adherents especially because reforms, reconstruction, development, and security have not "gained traction" across the country, particularly among the Pashtun-dominated regions.[11]

Afghanistan's drug economy is currently estimated to contribute around half of the gross domestic product of the country, more than US$3 billion. Afghanistan now produces around 92 per cent of world opium, making the country's economy a criminal economy.[12] The Taliban have used the opium economy as a source of rebuilding their

9. Korski, Daniel (2008). "MIA in Afghanistan", *Daily Times* (Lahore), 31 January.

10. Seale, Patrick (2006). "Losing the War in Afghanistan", *Daily Times*, 19 December.

11. See report by The Atlantic Council of the United States (2008). "Saving Afghanistan: A Plan and Appeal for Urgent Action", *Issue Brief*, International Security Program, 30 January. p.3.

12. See report by Anderson, Jon Lee (2007). "Letter from Afghanistan: The Taliban's Opium War; The Difficulties and Dangers of the Eradication Program", *The New Yorker*: 60-71, 9 and 16 July.

political roots in the Pashtun community. Much time, it seems, has been lost in winning over the Pashtun tribes through soft policies. Far from pacifying the Pashtun countryside the hard-hitting counter-insurgency blows have, however, caused a great deal of collateral damage. Additionally, human rights abuses and little output of the reconstruction efforts reaching the people have pushed them closer to the Taliban. After seven years of international assistance, waves of counter-insurgency campaigns, and political support, Afghanistan is still in the red zone. The new Afghan state has not taken off and remains merely symbolic, nominal, and deprived of social energies and broad-based legitimacy.

Conclusion

Every neighbour of Afghanistan facing a spectre of wider instability, and western countries that are concerned about the "bloody borders" of Islam, have a great stake in the reconstruction of Afghanistan as a stable, peaceful, unified nation-state. In terms of history, terrain, legacy and the nature of the task, Afghanistan poses one of the greatest challenges in post-conflict reconstruction. Failure of nation- and state-building in Afghanistan will imply disaster for the entire international community. This is one of those collaborative international efforts whose success will make every country a victor, and its failure every one a loser.

Afghanistan can be transformed from a centre-point of regional conflict to a nexus of regional cooperation. But this would require some cool analysis and evaluation of what has gone wrong, what policy instruments are needed for course correction and, more importantly, how international interest and support can be sustained over a long period of time. The Afghan leaders and the neighbouring states will have to show greater wisdom, assume more responsibility, and resolve imagined and real problems before a frustrated world community turns its back on the country. Afghanistan as a failed or nominal state is not in anyone's interest, particularly of the regional actors.

6

Pakistani Attitudes towards Militancy in and beyond Pakistan[1]

C. CHRISTINE FAIR[2]

Background to the Problem[3]

Prior to General Pervez Musharraf's acceptance of the US-given ultimatum to join the US-led global war on terrorism in September 2001, Pakistan's militant landscape could be meaningfully segregated by the group's sectarian orientation, its theatre of operation, and its ethnic constitution. For example, there were militant groups (*askari tanzeems*) that traditionally focused upon Kashmir, including the Deobandi groups of Jaish-e-Mohammad, Harkat-ul-Ansar/Harkat-ul-Mujahideen; Ahl-e-Hadith organisations such as Punjab-based Lashkar-e-Taiba; as well as groups operating under the influence of the Jamaat-e-Islami such as al-Badr and Hizbul Mujahideen, which tend to be comprised of Kashmiris. Other *askari tanzeems* (as Pakistanis often refer to the myriad militant groups operating in their country) have been traditionally sectarian in nature and include the anti-Shi'a Lashkar-e-Jhangvi and Sipah-e-Sahaba Pakistan.[4] Both are under the sway of the Deobandi organisation Jamiat-e-Ulema Islami (JUI) and

1. This essay was written in February 2007 and is based upon a recent poll fielded collaboratively by the author with Steven Kull and Clay Ramsay of PIPA. This survey was funded by the United States Institute of Peace. This work was undertaken while the author was with the USIP. She is now with the RAND Corporation. As such, the information cut-off for this essay is February 2007. Several surveys have been fielded subsequent to the USIP-backed effort and the findings presented here, fortunately, are stable. This essay represents her personal views and not those of USIP or RAND.

2. The author thanks Clay Ramsay and Steven Kull of PIPA for being superb collaborators.

3. This section draws from Fair, C. Christine (2008). "Who Are Pakistan's Militants and Their Families?" *Terrorism and Political Violence* (forthcoming) and Fair, C. Christine (2004). "Militant Recruitment in Pakistan: Implications for Al-Qa'ida and Other Organizations", *Studies in Conflict and Terrorism* 27(6) (November/December).

4. Many of these groups have been proscribed numerous times only to re-emerge. Many now operate under new names. This essay uses the names which are likely to be most familiar to readers.

are funded by wealthy Arab individuals and organisations. Notably, many of these Deobandi *tanzeems* have overlapping membership and they also have strong connections to the JUI.[5] In the past, Shi'a sectarian groups were also lethally active. These groups targeted Sunni Muslims and obtained funding from Iran, although these groups have largely disappeared.[6]

Since late 2001 and 2002, many of Pakistan's militant groups—particularly those of Deobandi background—have splintered and/or have reoriented in terms of targets and tactics. Many of the Deobandi groups are tightly allied to the Afghan and Pakistani Taliban, and are increasingly aiming their resources at the Pakistani state even though some elements within these same groups continue to enjoy various levels of formal and informal state support. While their targets have included President Musharraf, they have also included other high-value military and civilian leaders. Al-Qaeda leaders continue to operate and plan attacks from the tribal areas, including Osama bin Laden, Ayman al-Zawahiri, Abu Ubaidah al-Masri, and Abu al-Yazid. Recent attacks and plots—such as the successful July 2005 attack in London, transatlantic plot foiled in 2006, and plot to attack the US and German targets in 2007—have connections back to Pakistan's Pashtun belt. Since 2006, militants have launched sanguinary suicide attacks against Pakistan's national security establishment, including the Frontier Corps, intelligence services, and the army. While the actual numbers of suicide attacks dramatically increased in 2007, the aforenoted innovation in targeting seems to have occurred in 2006 in response to the US attacks on sites in Bajaur.[7]

5. Zahab, Mariam Abou and Olivier Roy (2004). *Islamist Networks: The Afghan-Pakistan Connection*. London: C. Hurst; Fair, C. Christine (2004). "Militant Recruitment in Pakistan: Implications for Al-Qa'ida and Other Organizations", *Studies in Conflict and Terrorism* 27: 489–504 (November/December).

6. Since the onset of sanguinary sectarian violence in Iraq and Iran's 2006 victory in Lebanon, it has been suspected that Iran may once again be involved in inciting anti-Sunni violence in Pakistan. Indeed throughout 2007, Pakistan has seen a sharp increase in sectarian violence compared to 2006 or previous years. However, the overwhelming preponderance of those attacks has been perpetrated by anti-Shi'a militias. Thus, the allegations of Iran's involvement are not supported empirically at this point.

7. For example, on 5 November 2007, a suicide attacker assaulted army recruits doing exercises in north-west Pakistan, killing at least 41 soldiers and wounding dozens. This attack was reportedly in retaliation for the US strike on a purported *madrasa* on 30 October 2007 which killed 82 persons. See Constable, Pamela and Kamran Khan (2006). "Suicide Bombing Kills 41 Troops at Pakistani Army Base: Attack Called Reprisal for Strike on School", *Washington Post*, 9 November, at <*www.washingtonpost.com/wp-dyn/content/article/2006/11/08/AR2006110800397.html*>

In recent years, Pakistan has witnessed the development of a militancy whose activists describe themselves as "Pakistani Taliban" (Tehreek-e-Taliban-e-Pakistan or TTP). The rise of this movement seems to have coincided with or was precipitated by the Pakistani military operations in the Federally Administered Tribal Areas (FATA). While the Pakistan army undertook military operations in the northern tribal agencies in 2002 in support of the US operations in Afghanistan, those early operations were successfully executed without significant repercussions. However, Pakistan's operations in Waziristan, which commenced in the south in the spring of 2004 and which focused upon foreign elements, were conducted with varying degrees of success and many failures.

Since 2001, Pakistan has lost at least 1400 troops (including the army, paramilitary forces such as the Frontier Corps, and police).[8] Since 2004, the army has suffered several defeats, witnessed several bouts of humiliating surrenders to the Taliban, and has ratified several defeats through various formal deals with Taliban elements in North and South Waziristan. Episodic US strikes (as in Bajaur since January 2006 and intensifying throughout 2008) coupled with these Pakistani military inadequacies have fostered a widespread Islamist insurgency along the Afghan border with self-styled local Taliban establishing parallel systems of governance under purported Sharia rule. Since 2004, Pakistan has also witnessed the resurgence of al-Qaeda and concomitant "Pakistanisation" of al-Qaeda.

While the Talibanisation of the tribal areas was initially limited to North and South Waziristan, the phenomenon next spread to Bajaur. Most recently, the Pakistani Taliban have emerged in areas that had previously been peaceful, such as Mohmand agency, Orakzai, and Kurram. They have also emerged in the frontier areas of Bannu, Tank, Kohat, Lakki Marwar, Dera Ismil Khan, and Swat. Throughout the summer of 2007, the Frontier Corps (along with the Frontier Constabulary) battled the Pakistani militants associated with the Tehreek-e-Nafaz-e-Shariat-e-Mohammadi, who seized the Swat Valley

8. While US officials routinely acknowledge Pakistan's losses, it is difficult to assess the accuracy of these figures. Throughout 2008, Pakistan's operations in Bajaur in particular have accounted for mounting casualties for the armed forces. Thus, this number may be a significant undercounting of actual losses.

in late October.[9] The valley was finally wrested from the militants when elements from the 11th Corps entered the fray. Pakistan's armed forces remain engaged in Swat.[10] The reach of these groups also extends to Islamabad, as attested to by Taliban supporters who were ensconced in the Lal Masjid until the Pakistani security forces launched Operation Silence in July 2007 to oust them.[11] As many of the students in the associated *madaris* (pl. *madrasa*) were from Swat and Chitral, the backlash from this operation was witnessed in those areas and indeed the Swat crisis may have been precipitated by Operation Silence.

Some analysts fear that this insurgency, while politically framed in Islamist terms, has become a more generalised Pashtun insurgency mobilising supporters based upon local Pashtun grievances in various localities; threat perceptions of the Pakistani state; the international presence in Afghanistan; and apprehensions about the legitimacy of the Afghan and Pakistan governments under US-allied Presidents Karzai and Musharraf. Given that the Pakistan army lacks the counter-insurgency skills needed to combat the threat there and the Frontier Corps is under-equipped, poorly trained, and deeply compromised, the prospects for halting this movement are slim. Worse yet, the Pakistani polity has not embraced Pakistan's counterterrorism and counter-insurgency (COIN) efforts. Without political support, Pakistan's leadership will be unable to wage COIN effectively.

Because Pakistani public attitudes towards these efforts are critical to Pakistan's ability and political will to stay involved in COIN operations, this chapter explores several important clusters of Pakistani public attitudes, including their support for and threat perceptions of

---

9. Fair, Christine (2007). "Pakistan Loses Swat to Local Taliban", *Terrorism Focus* 4(37).
10. There is very little scholarly literature on this phenomenon, with most coverage taking place in the popular press or security publications. See, *inter alia*, Yusufzai, Rahimullah (2007). "The Emergence of the Pakistani Taliban", *Jane's Information Group*, 11 December, at <*www8.janes.com*>. See also Fair, C. Christine. "Pakistan Loses Swat to Local Taliban", n.8; Abbas, Hassan (2007). "Is the NWFP Slipping out of Pakistan's Control?" *Terrorism Monitor* 5(22); Abbas, Hassan (2007). "Increasing Talibanisation in Pakistan's Seven Tribal Agencies", *Terrorism Monitor* 5(18); Bakhtiar, Idrees (2007). "Between the Lines", *The Herald*, July; Khan, Ghafar Ali (2007). "The Lost Frontier", *The Herald*, July; Tohid, Owais (2004). "The New Frontier", *Newsline*, April; Tohid, Owais (2004). "The Warrior Tribes", *Newsline*, April; Hussain, Zahid (2004). "Al-Qaeda's New Face", *Newsline*, August.
11. Hussain, Zahid (2007). "The Battle for the Soul of Pakistan", *Newsline*, July, at <*www.newsline.com.pk/NewsJul2007/cover1july2007.htm*>

a variety of militant groups operating in and from Pakistan; support for the Pakistan government's handling of various crises and public policies related to militancy; beliefs about the government's ties to militant groups; and perceived benefits from the various groups. To do so, it employs data collected in the summer of 2007 in a study commissioned by the author under the auspices of the United States Institute of Peace (USIP) in collaboration with the Program on International Policy Attitudes (PIPA).[12] After briefly describing the USIP data employed here, the remainder of the chapter first explores data that broadly address the degree to which Pakistanis have supported various forms of violence and the degree to which they perceive a wide array of militant groups as threats to Pakistani security.

The USIP-PIPA Dataset

The author, working under the auspices of USIP, in collaboration with research staff from PIPA, developed a comprehensive questionnaire to probe Pakistani public opinion on a wide array of domestic and foreign policy concerns. These questions pertain to their attitudes to numerous militant groups operating in Pakistan, including al-Qaeda, the Taliban, various *askari tanzeems* engaged over Kashmir, sectarian militant groups, and ethnic militant movements such as the insurgency in Baluchistan and previous conflicts in Sindh. Questions to ascertain views about policy issues covered the government's handling of the crisis in FATA and at the Red Mosque, among other public policies. The instrument also queried respondents' opinions about several kinds of militant targets (e.g., Indian police, women and children of armed forces personnel, civilian targets such as parliament and national assemblies). The survey was conducted from 12 to 18 September, just before President Pervez Musharraf declared a six-week state of emergency and before the assassination of Benazir Bhutto. The sample included 907 Pakistani urban adults, selected using multi-stage probability sampling, who were interviewed at home in 19 cities across

12. For a presentation of the basic findings, see Fair, C. Christine Steven Kull and Clay Ramsay (2008). *Pakistani Public Opinion on Democracy, Islamist Militancy, and Relations with the US*. Washington DC: PIPA/USIP. 7 January.

all of Pakistan's provinces. The margin of error is +/– 3.3 per cent.[13] The bulk of this chapter derives from analyses of these data.

Pakistani Threat Perceptions of and Support for Militant Activities

Unfortunately, there are relatively few robust data sources that provide insights into Pakistani public attitudes about militancy and the groups that engage in violence. One important source of such information is the Pew Foundation, which has been surveying Pakistan since early 2002 as a part of the Global Attitudes Survey. For several years, Pew has asked the below-given question in Pakistan and several other countries to measure support for suicide terrorism and other attacks against civilians to defend Islam:

> Some people think that suicide bombing and other forms of violence against civilian targets are justified in order to defend Islam from its enemies. Other people believe that, no matter what the reason, this kind of violence is never justified. Do you personally feel that this kind of violence is often justified to defend Islam, sometimes justified, rarely justified, or never justified?

When Pew first fielded this question to a largely national sample in 2002, one-third of the sample (33 per cent) believed that such attacks were often or sometimes justified.[14] In March 2004, this number actually increased to 41 per cent.[15] In 2005, this figure declined to 25 per cent[16] and to 14 per cent in 2006.[17] By 2007, only 9 per cent believed that such attacks were always or sometimes justified[18] (see Figure 6.1).

---

13. Ibid.

14. The Pew Research Center for the People and the Press (2002). "2002 Global Attitudes Survey, Final Topline", 4 December, at <*pewglobal.org/reports/pdf/165topline.pdf*>

15. The Pew Research Center for the People and the Press (2004). "Nine Nation Survey (March 2004), Final Top Line", 16 March, at <*pewglobal.org/reports/pdf/206topline.pdf*>

16. The Pew Research Center for the People and the Press (2005). "Pew Global Attitudes Project, Spring 2005, 17-Nation Survey", 14 July, at <*pewglobal.org/reports/pdf/248topline.pdf*>

17. The Pew Research Center for the People and the Press (2007). "Pew Global Attitudes Project: Spring 2007 Survey. Survey of 47 Publics. Final 2007 Trends Topline", 24 July, at <*pewglobal.org/reports/pdf/257topline-trend.pdf*>

18. Ibid.

Figure 6.1

Pakistani Support for Suicide Bombings: Per cent Who Say "Always or Sometimes Justified"

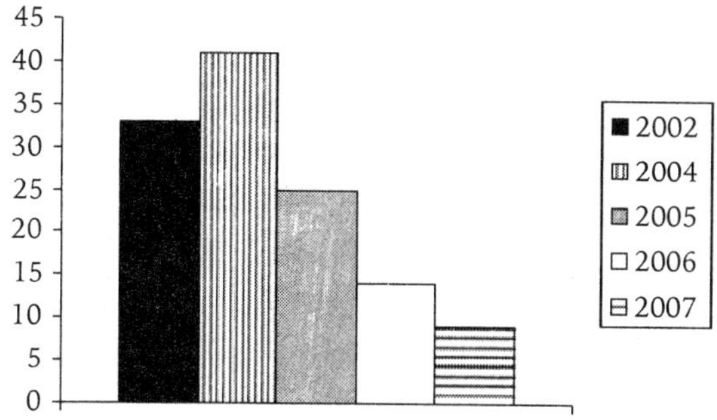

The USIP/PIPA team asked a question similar to that used by Pew and obtained similar results. When the USIP/PIPA team posed the below question, 15 per cent indicated that such attacks are often or sometimes justified. Some two-thirds (66 per cent) said they were rarely or never justified. (20 per cent did not answer.)

> Some people think that bombing and other types of attacks intentionally aimed at civilians are sometimes justified while others think that this kind of violence is never justified. Do you personally feel that such attacks are often justified, sometimes justified, rarely justified, or never justified?

Note that while the question is similar, the USIP/PIPA question does not specifically mention suicide bombings. This—along with different sample structures and temporal affects—may explain the difference between the USIP/PIPA and Pew results.

While such questions have a general usefulness, previous survey work by the author and PIPA in Iran found that it is most useful to query respondents about particular groups of actors and targets rather than general and broad statements about violence. The USIP/PIPA team asked respondents about a series of militant groups operating in and from Pakistan, and whether these groups posed a threat to Pakistan. The survey team provided respondents with a list of groups in Pakistan that conduct various activities. For each one, the respondent indicated whether she or he sees "these activities as a threat or not to the vital interests of Pakistan in the next ten years". Respondents were asked about the "Activities of Sindhi nationalists in Pakistan"; "Activities of Mohajir nationalists in Pakistan"; "Activities of Baluch nationalists in Pakistan"; "Activities of Islamist militants and local Taliban in FATA and settled areas"; "Activities of al-Qaeda"; and "Activities of *askari tanzeems* in Pakistan".

As the data in Table 6.1 demonstrate, Pakistanis do distinguish across these different groups with ethnic nationalists (Sindhi, Mohajir, and Baluch) registering far less concern than do Islamist militants (e.g., local Taliban, al-Qaeda and the *askari tanzeems*). In fact, a plurality finds the Islamist militants to pose critical threats to the state's vital interests, and solid majorities believe that they are either a critical or important threat. This certainly suggests that many urban Pakistanis are not insouciant about these groups or even supportive as is sometimes suggested in the media. While this is certainly encouraging, there are important minorities (14–18 per cent) who do not find these groups to be a threat at all.

Table 6.1

Pakistani Threat Perceptions of a Range of Militant Groups (in per cent)

Group	*Yes, Critical Threat*	*Yes, an Important, but not a Critical Threat*	*Not a Threat*	*Refused/ Don't Know*
Activities of Sindhi nationalists in Pakistan	18	28	41	13
Activities of Mohajir nationalists in Pakistan	22	33	32	13
Activities of Baluch nationalists in Pakistan	17	26	41	17
Activities of Islamist militants and local Taliban in FATA and settled areas	34	26	18	22
Activities of al-Qaeda	41	21	14	24
Activities of *askari tanzeems* in Pakistan	38	23	17	22

As noted above, many Pakistanis do believe that *askari tanzeems* do present critical threats to Pakistan's vital interests. However, as the below-given data indicate, many Pakistanis also believe that they advance the security of Kashmiris in Indian-administered Kashmir. Thus while they may threaten Pakistan, clearly they are seen to have some value when operating outside of Pakistan and in Kashmir. To probe further the kind of legitimacy that these groups' actions enjoy among Pakistanis in the context of Kashmir, we put forth the following question to respondents:

> In the context of the conflict in occupied Kashmir, for each of the following types of people, please tell me if you think that attacks against them are often justified, sometimes justified, rarely justified, or never justified?

We included in the list Indian policemen, Indian intelligence agents, Indian military and paramilitary troops, Indian government officials, women and children of the military, and women and children more generally. As the data in Table 6.2 indicate, nearly one in five believed that attacks against Indian policemen, intelligence agencies, and police and paramilitary troops are often justified. When one includes the "sometime justified" categories, support for such targets is as high as 40 per cent. Support for attacks against Indian government officials was somewhat lower with only one in four believing they were often or sometimes justified. Overwhelmingly, Pakistanis rejected wives and children as legitimate targets—even those associated with the military.

Table 6.2

Pakistani Support for Militant Targets (in the Context of Kashmir) (in per cent)

Target	*Often Justified*	*Sometimes Justified*	*Rarely Justified*	*Never Justified*	*Refused/ Don't Know*
Indian policemen	18	20	14	35	13
Indian intelligence agents	19	17	16	34	14
Indian military and paramilitary troops	19	20	15	33	13
Indian government officials	11	14	19	41	16
Wives and children of the military	1	2	8	75	15
Women and children	1	1	7	76	15

While the above set of questions focused upon the context of Kashmir, we also asked more general questions about the legitimacy of targets, including "government institutions (like the national Parliament in Delhi and state assemblies)"; "Attacks conducted against Indian targets like subways, stock exchanges, and tourist sites"; "Attacks in India on families of Indian military personnel"; "Attacks in Pakistan on Shi'a"; and "Attacks in Pakistan on Ahmediyya".

Among the "Indian" targets, levels of support are somewhat consistent—albeit lower—than the Kashmir-specific targets. Support for attacks against government institutions, civilian infrastructure, and attacks on Indian military personnel within India are deemed "sometimes justified" by 15 per cent, 12 per cent, and 13 per cent of respondents respectively. Support for harming Pakistani targets (Shi'a, and Ahmediyya, which have been subject to decades of vilification in Pakistan) is much lower at 5 and 6 per cent. Pakistani respondents appear to differentiate among these targets with substantially more support when groups target persons and institutions in India. This support also seems to increase when the violence is in the context of the Kashmir dispute.

Table 6.3

Pakistani Support for Militant Targets (in per cent)

Target	*Sometimes Justified*	*Never Justified*	*Refused/ Don't Know*
Attacks conducted against government institutions (like the national Parliament in Delhi and state assemblies)	15	64	21
Attacks conducted against Indian targets like subways, stock exchanges, and tourist sites	12	68	20
Attacks in India on families of Indian military personnel	13	67	19
Attacks in Pakistan on Shi'a	5	78	17
Attacks in Pakistan on Ahmediyya	6	75	19

It is widely believed outside of Pakistan that some of the *askari tanzeems* do target civilians even if their preferred target is military, police or intelligence. We asked Pakistani respondents to consider whether Jaish-e-Mohammad, Hizbul Mujahideen, and Lashkar-e-Taiba deliberately target civilians. Majorities simply refused to answer the question or claimed to have no opinion. However, across the three *tanzeems*, only 6 per cent said that the group in question "has intentionally targeted citizens". Given the preponderance of media accounts about such attacks on civilians, this low number is rather surprising. Recall LeT's famed attack on wives and children at

Kaluchak in May 2002, which was widely reported with LeT explicitly claiming that attack in its own publications.

The team also asked a number of questions about the Taliban. As is well known, one of Washington's concerns about Pakistan is the sanctuary that the Taliban forces enjoy in Pakistan. As the Taliban were the clients of the Pakistani state for several years and given that the reversal encountered some resistance, the team wanted to explore Pakistani beliefs about the Taliban and its activities.

The team first queried respondent beliefs about Taliban activities by asking them to think about "attacks by the Taliban against NATO [western] troops in Afghanistan" and indicate whether they "approve of them, disapprove of them, or have mixed feelings about them? Do you feel that way somewhat or strongly?" Thirty per cent strongly or somewhat approved. Only 15 per cent disapproved and another 18 per cent had "mixed feelings". (The remaining 37 per cent were refusals or "do not know" responses.)

Next they were asked about "Attacks by the Taliban against Afghan troops and police in Afghanistan". Only 5 per cent strongly approved and another 13 per cent approved somewhat. In contrast, 29 per cent disapproved somewhat or strongly while 14 per cent had "mixed feelings". (The remaining 38 per cent did not provide an affirmative response.)

These responses suggest that Pakistanis are far more likely to condone Taliban activities when they target western forces and much more apprehensive to do so when the victims are Afghan forces.

Pakistani Support for the Government's Handling of Militancy

With respect to Pakistan's domestic security, the data in Table 6.1 demonstrate that many Pakistanis do perceive these groups to imperil Pakistan. However, there is considerable discord among Pakistanis about the way in which the government has handled issues germane to these groups. To probe support for the government's various public policies, the survey team asked respondents to indicate whether they "approve strongly, approve somewhat, disapprove somewhat, or disapprove strongly of the way Pakistan's government is handling the following issues". The team probed beliefs about the situations in Indian-administered Kashmir, FATA, and the Lal Masjid.

As the data in Table 6.4 demonstrate, with respect to the government's handling of Indian-administered Kashmir, solid majorities approve of the government's approach and nearly one in three approve strongly. With respect to FATA, there is considerable ambivalence with 48 per cent either approving strongly or somewhat and 34 per cent disapproving somewhat or strongly. Support for the government's handling of the Lal Masjid is even lower, with 31 per cent lending some degree of support while a majority disapproves.

Table 6.4

Pakistani Support for Government Policies (in per cent)

Policy	*Approve Strongly*	*Approve Somewhat*	*Disapprove Some*	*Disapprove Strongly*	*Refused/ Don't Know*
The situation in Indian-admin Kashmir	32	36	13	9	9
The situation in the FATA	14	34	22	12	18
Religious extremism such as the Lal Masjid	12	19	27	29	13

The international community has become acutely concerned about developments in FATA both because of the import for the international efforts to rehabilitate Afghanistan, and because major terror conspiracies in Europe and the United States have important linkages to militant groups ensconced in FATA. As noted above, the data suggest considerable ambivalence about Pakistan's approach in FATA. To obtain a more granular understanding of public preferences for FATA, we offered respondents three statements about FATA (Federally Administered Tribal Areas) and asked which "comes closer to your view?" The statements are given below:

Statement A: Pakistan's government should exert control over FATA, even if it means using military force to do so.

Statement B: The government should not try to exert control over FATA but should try to keep the peace through negotiating deals with local Taliban.

Statement C: The government should withdraw its forces from FATA and leave the people alone.

The plurality (46 per cent) believed that "B" (keep peace through negotiating) best represented their view. Nearly one in four believed that "A" (military force if needed to control FATA) best accorded with their preference. A small minority (12 per cent) identified "C" (withdraw forces and leave the people alone). Only 18 per cent declined to provide an answer. This seems to suggest that the least objectionable aspect of Pakistan's approach to FATA has been negotiating deals brokered with the militants.

Pakistanis are somewhat more accepting of Pakistani military action when the target is al-Qaeda. Respondents were asked whether or not they favour or oppose the Pakistani army entering FATA to pursue and capture al-Qaeda fighters. While 44 per cent said they favoured the policy, 36 per cent said that they oppose it.

Similar results were obtained when asked about hot pursuit of Taliban insurgents who have crossed over from Afghanistan. Nearly half (48 per cent) favoured allowing the Pakistan army to pursue and capture Taliban insurgents who have crossed into Pakistan. However, more than one in three (34 per cent) opposed it.

Pakistanis were also not enthusiastic about the prospects of capturing Osama bin Laden. Participants were asked "Suppose the Pakistani government learned that Osama bin Laden was in FATA and found his exact location. Do you think then that the government should or should not attempt to capture him?" While nearly one in four (24 per cent) believed that they should capture him, a plurality (30 per cent) opposed this. (The rest did not provide an answer.)

Such ambivalence may be due in part to the fact that few Pakistanis believe that Osama bin Laden is in Pakistan (2 per cent). In contrast, 18 per cent believe that he is in Afghanistan. (Most respondents simply opted not to provide an answer and 8 per cent even volunteered that he is in the United States.)

As expected, there is near universal opposition (80 per cent) to allowing the Americans or other foreign troops to enter Pakistan to pursue and capture al-Qaeda, and similar levels of opposition (77 per cent) for those troops to engage in hot pursuit of Taliban figures crossing into Pakistan from Afghanistan.

While the military component of the policy may be unpopular, another survey item found that Pakistanis do support political reform for FATA. When asked whether they supported leaving the colonial-era and draconian Frontier Crimes Regulation (FCR) unchanged, modifying it "slowly over time such that the people there should have the same rights and responsibilities as all other Pakistanis", or abolishing it such that the people there should have the same rights and responsibilities as all other Pakistanis", only a slim minority (8 per cent) favoured leaving the FCR intact. The largest percentage (46 per cent) favoured modification and more than one in four favoured abolishing it altogether. Thus while there may be ambivalence about the government's policy of military action, appeasement of the militants and political reform seems quite palatable. Unfortunately, while Islamabad has episodically embraced policies of appeasement of the militants it is loath to consider political reforms.

Beliefs of the Government's Involvement in Militant Activities

Many in the South Asian region and beyond believe that Pakistan's intelligence agencies have long supported—and continue to support—a large number of militant groups operating in Pakistan, Afghanistan, Indian-administered Kashmir, and elsewhere in India. Given Pakistanis' threat perception and the ultimate objective of the USIP/PIPA study to determine whether or not Pakistanis view the war on terror as their own, the team probed respondent beliefs about the relationship between these groups and various Pakistani agencies.

With respect to *askari tanzeems* (such as Jaish-e-Mohammad, Hizbol Mujahideen and Lashkar-e-Taiba), we asked respondents to identify from a list of options that which "best describes the relationship, if any, between these groups and the Pakistani army and intelligence agencies". While 51 per cent refused or claimed to not know, one in four believed that "There is no relationship at all". Fourteen per cent believed that "There are some contacts". Five per cent selected "Some elements within the army and intelligence agencies provide support such as money, training, advice and weapons" and another 5 per cent identified "The army and intelligence services as a whole work closely with these groups". Taken together, among those who volunteered an answer, respondents are ambivalent, with as many believing there are no connections (25 per cent) as there are those who believe there is some kind of government involvement (24 per cent).

Regarding the Taliban, we asked respondents whether they think that "the Pakistan government is seriously trying to stop the Taliban from operating in Afghanistan, or is it allowing the Taliban to operate in Afghanistan?" While a plurality of respondents (36 per cent refused to answer or did not know), one in three respondents believed that the government is "seriously trying to stop the Taliban from operating in Afghanistan." Only 7 per cent believed it was "allowing" or "helping" the Taliban operate in Afghanistan. (The remaining sample offered "depends" (12 per cent) and "neither" (13 per cent).) Clearly, most Pakistanis who answered the question believe that their government is seeking to retard the Taliban, a view which does not accord with views in the United States, Afghanistan or NATO-contributing countries.

We next queried participants about government support for groups operating in Indian-administered Kashmir (or Occupied Kashmir as Pakistanis refer to the area). We asked respondents whether they "think the Pakistani government does or does not give weapons and money to some militant groups that fight in the Indian-controlled region of Occupied Kashmir". The largest group (47 per cent) were in the refused/don't know category. However, the next-largest group (40 per cent) believed that it "Does not give weapons and money." Only 13 per cent believed that the government "Does give weapons and money." This view too is discordant with popular beliefs about these issues outside of Pakistan.

Perceived Benefits Derived from Militant Activities and Groups

Individuals may support specific groups or at least decline to view their activities as a threat if such persons perceive that the group or its actions confer benefits to that person, her or her community or to the state of Pakistan. Similarly, persons who believe that such groups and their actions impose harm may be less likely to support them and to identify them as threats.

To explore different kinds of perceived benefits, we asked respondents several questions about groups, their actions and their impacts.

As noted above, while many Pakistanis see *askari tanzeems* as a threat, fewer identified these groups other than the Taliban or al-Qaeda. The team asked respondents to consider "Pakistani militant groups [*askari tanzeem*] that operate in Occupied Kashmir" and to indicate whether they "think that, on balance, they help Pakistan's security, hurt Pakistan's security, or have no effect either way on Pakistan's security". While the largest group declined to provide an answer (39 per cent), nearly one in five believed that they "Help Pakistan's security", which was somewhat higher than the percentage who believed that they "Hurt Pakistan's security" (17 per cent). Somewhat more than one in four believed that they "Have no effect either way."

We also asked respondents whether "these groups help the security of people in Occupied Kashmir, hurt it, or have no effect either way". Again, a high percentage (37 per cent) declined to provide an answer. However, the largest group (39 per cent) believed that they "Help Kashmiris' security." In contrast, only 9 per cent believed that they "Hurt Kashmiris' security."

Finally, the team asked respondents to think about "groups like Lashkar-e-Taiba, Jamaat-ul Dawa, Hizbul Mujahideen, and Jaish-e-Mohammad among other *tanzeems*, do you think they provide social and community services, or are these not part of their activities?" While more than one in three refused to answer, the largest group (42 per cent) did not believe that they offered such services. Nonetheless, nearly one in four did believe they offered social and community services.

For the 23 per cent of the sample who did think these militant groups offered such services, the team asked them to "mention a few services you are aware of". (Multiple responses were permitted.) As the data in Table 6.5 suggest, respondents identified *madaris* and other schools along with medical care, humanitarian assistance, and financial help with marriages and burials as forms of assistance.

Table 6.5

Services Believed to be Provided by Pakistani Militant Groups

Service	*Per cent*
Deeni Madrasas	22
Schools that are not *deeni madrasas*	15
Medical care or services	16
Humanitarian assistance during floods, earthquakes, famine	19
Financial help with marriage and burials	11
Refused/Don't know	29

Conclusions and Implications

While these data offer many encouraging insights about the degree to which a majority of Pakistanis view most militant groups as a decisive threat, there are important minorities who do not feel threatened by them and consistent minorities who justify a wide array of militant activities. Pakistanis are more likely to justify specific attacks in the contexts of Kashmir and India, and attacks in Afghanistan targeting Western forces. The Pakistani polity, however, is ambivalent about the government's military policies towards the Taliban and towards such events as the Lal Masjid. At the same time, policies of negotiating with the militants in the FATA and political reform are popular while policies of military confrontation are less so. Military confrontation of foreign elements (e.g., al-Qaeda and Taliban fugitives in Pakistan who come across from Afghanistan) is more popular although important and sizeable minorities still oppose such operations against these foreign, infiltrating targets. The US and other foreign military operations are deeply opposed even when the targets are foreign and seeking refuge in Pakistan from Afghanistan. The US officials who have discussed such unilateral action should be cautioned by these results as such commentary has been inflammatory. As noted, US unilateral action in Bajaur galvanised a wider militancy beyond FATA and likely precipitated the induction of suicide strikes against Pakistani troops in FATA in 2006. Taken together, these results do not suggest that Pakistanis have embraced the war on terrorism as their own even though majorities view various militant groups as posing a threat to Pakistan's own vital interests.

Indeed, when respondents were queried about the US-Pakistan relationship that has developed after 9/11, few believe the relationship has "mostly benefited Pakistan" (6 per cent). The largest group (44 per cent) believed that it has "mostly benefited the United States". (Twelve per cent thought both states equally benefited and another 11 per cent thought neither benefited. More than one in four declined to answer.) Other questions revealed that most Pakistanis are deeply dubious of the United States and its actions. Some 73 per cent believed that spreading Christianity was "definitely" or "probably" a goal of the United States, and 78 per cent believed that maintaining control of the resources of the Middle East was "definitely" or "probably" a US goal. Another 86 per cent believed that weakening and dividing the Muslim world was "definitely" or "probably" a US goal. In fact, many Pakistanis (likely with great justification) may believe that they are a victim of terrorism because of the US-Pakistan military alliance rather than a *sui generis* blow-back from Pakistan's past policies.

The policy puzzle that emerges from this effort is how the international community and indeed anti-militant elements within the Pakistani government can support the large majorities of Pakistanis who feel threatened by the various militant groups while at the same time mobilising them to embrace the war on terrorism as a conflict for Pakistan's own survival as a modern and moderate Muslim state.

Unfortunately, for many years, Musharraf repeatedly explained in public and in private that Pakistan has sacrificed much—including the lives of many hundreds of armed services and police personal—for the US global war on terrorism. The US officials—in public and private—thanked him for his sacrifices. This was unfortunate. As early as 2001, the US officials should have consistently encouraged the Pakistani leadership publicly and privately to embrace the notion that Pakistan is waging its own war on terrorism to secure the future Pakistan that is desired by most Pakistanis. Instead, the United States bolstered the belief among the Pakistani leadership and the polity that indeed President Musharraf was waging a war on behalf of Washington and President Bush. This perception that President Musharraf was doing the bidding of President Bush was unpopular among Pakistanis and gave rise to humorous monikers for the two leaders such as "Busharraf".

It was not until late 2005 and early 2006 that Musharraf began expounding the notion that Pakistan is waging a war for its own sovereignty and its own standing as a moderate Muslim nation. Presumably, these statements were too late and unpersuasive. How could Musharraf reverse narratives and convince Pakistanis that the nation was fighting for its national survival, not his own personal survival? By 2005, Musharraf's own standing had been vitiated by his personal desire to remain on as President and Chief of Army Staff despite the increasing criticism of the extra-constitutionality of his dual-hats coming from an ever-broadening base of critics.

Under the current political conditions, Musharraf is ever more unlikely to be able or willing to mobilise Pakistanis in their own war on terrorism when, according to a mid-January Gallup Poll, nearly half of Pakistanis surveyed believed that government agencies or government-linked politicians killed Benazir Bhutto. Only 17 per cent believed that Bhutto was killed by the Taliban or al-Qaeda.[19] With the near-certitude of massive electoral irregularities, elections do not offer encouragement that a credible leader will emerge who can galvanise public support for a state effort to crack down on militancy in the country.

Finally, while there are extreme crises of civilian leadership in Pakistan and pervasive ambivalence about the influence of militant groups in Pakistan, the largest obstacle to a Pakistan committed to the war on terrorism is the view of the strategic elite. At this juncture, there is no robust evidence that the state has made a strategic decision to abandon the use of militants for domestic and foreign policy objectives. Reporting in June and July of 2007 does suggest that there is—at long last—a difference of opinion among these elites with growing numbers of persons who believe that these proxies pose more harm than good. Moreover, it is widely believed that the Pakistan army is confronting a serious morale problem having waged military operations against its own citizens as well as foreign elements with numerous setbacks for years. The challenge remains how to galvanise those sceptics of the militants' long-term utility, sideline those committed proponents of proxy elements, and mobilise the important

19. Associated Press (2008). "Pakistanis Suspect Officials Tied to Bhutto Death: Nearly Half Blamed Either Government Agencies or Rival Politicians", 13 January, at <*http://www.msnbc.msn.com/id/22635311/*>

majority of Pakistanis against these groups. Without successfully managing these three feats, the future of Pakistan and the region augurs greater instability with ever more important security threats beyond the borders of South Asia.

7

Taking Stock of the Afghan Conflict

External-Internal Dimensions

SHANTHIE MARIET D'SOUZA

The Security Situation

Afghanistan in 2008 saw a record level of violence. Seven years after the initiation of the US-led military action, violence and insecurity prevails in wide swathes of the southern Afghanistan. The Taliban influence has increased in southern provinces with the avowed objective of strategic encirclement of Kabul this year. According to NATO sources, the Taliban have concentrated forces in the southern, eastern and western provinces—Helmand, Kandahar, Farah, Uruzgan, Nangrahar, Ghazni, Zabul, Paktika, Khost, and Ghor.[1] Afghan security forces and international forces continue their positional warfare and direct combat with the Taliban in the south, east, and west. The geographic scope of Taliban activities has also widened with increased violence and instability in the Badghis, Mazar, Balkh, and Kunduz provinces, and the western Herat and Farah provinces.

Taliban Presence and Spread of Influence

The Taliban insurgency is notably different from the pre-9/11 monolithic entity. It is today a composition of loosely affiliated, amorphous, and diffused units under the Taliban umbrella. There are now multiple networks comprised of substantial anti-government forces: neo-Taliban guerrillas; followers of Gulbuddin Hekmatyar's radical group, Hizb-i-Islami; the Haqqani network; al-Qaeda and its affiliates; religious clerics; narcotic traffickers; anti-government armed groups; tribal

1. Synovitz, Ron (2007). "Afghanistan: Taliban Attacks Signal Start Of Spring Offensive", *Eurasianet*, 25 February, at <*http://www.eurasianet.org/departments/insight/articles/pp022507.shtml*> (accessed 1 February 2008).

fighters; and self-interested spoilers in the Pakistani tribal areas. The Taliban-led insurgency or the neo-Taliban began their activities in the spring of 2002 with the objective of overthrowing the interim Afghan government, and coerce the withdrawal of US and coalition forces by inflicting heavy losses on them. In many newer areas, the neo-Taliban have enlisted the support of disgruntled, disenchanted, and marginalised tribes and communities. Most of these groups may not share the political goals of the neo-Taliban, but they do share a common agenda in curtailing or limiting the writ of the state authority.

The Taliban-led groups are acting as "strategic spoilers",[2] seeking to discredit and undermine the Afghan government by targeting the coalition forces, officials and President Karzai's support base in the Pushtun Durrani tribal area. Suicide attacks, roadside bombing and beheading of hostages—all techniques al-Qaeda perfected in Iraq—are being employed by the Taliban to strengthen their influence and create pervasive insecurity. The attacks include a wide variety of operations targeting the US, coalition and Afghan security forces, as well as against Afghan and international civilians, mostly relying on asymmetric tactics. Over the years, however, the Taliban have switched between guerrilla tactics to positional warfare depending upon the strength of the opposition.

The strength of the neo-Taliban now stems as well from its gradual transformation to tech-savvy insurgents. Unlike the old Taliban movement, which denounced the use of modern technology, photography and mass communication, the neo-Taliban have a more sophisticated propaganda machine, including a video arm that seeks to manipulate international public opinion particularly in troop-contributing NATO countries. The Taliban's priority is "mobilisation of Muslim opinion worldwide as a source of funding, moral support and volunteers."[3]

Internal and External Support

An insurgency unable to generate sufficient external and internal

2. Kilcullen, David (2006). "Counterinsurgency Redux", *Survival* 48(4): 4 (Winter).
3. Giustozzi, Antonio (2008). *Koran, Kalashnikov and Laptop: The Neo-Taliban Insurgency in Afghanistan*. New York: Columbia University Press. p.138.

support fails to grow and even survive. Internal support provides legitimacy to the insurgent's agenda and equips it with intelligence, resources, infrastructure, security, and the recruits it needs to regenerate and expand its base.[4] Despite the early claims of successful completion of the Bonn process, the Afghan polity today represents fractured political processes, inadequate reconstruction, rising instability, and an alienated populace which continues to provide a support base to the insurgency.

The insurgency's external sponsor has provided it with sanctuaries and havens in its territory. A significant portion of the Afghan insurgency's military and political leadership is based in Pakistan. Insurgencies with well-established infrastructures and base areas, which can operate in protective terrain, cannot be quickly defeated.[5] The central goals of Operation Enduring Freedom (OEF)—the destruction of terrorist training camps and infrastructure within Afghanistan, the neutralisation of the al-Qaeda–Taliban combine, and the cessation of terrorist activities in Afghanistan[6]—are yet to yield tangible results mainly because of the "marginal" role played by Pakistan in the global war on terror (GWOT).

The insurgents have used Pakistan as a staging area for offensive operations in Afghanistan. Western intelligence sources have identified insurgent crossing points along the Afghan–Pakistani border.[7] The borders along Zabul and Kandahar are currently being used as the main ingress routes by the Taliban–al-Qaeda to infiltrate into Kandahar, Uruzgan, and Helmand provinces. The insurgents have significant support networks in Pakistan's North-West Frontier Province (NWFP) and Balochistan. Foreign jihadis operating in the provinces of Paktia and Paktika have found support across the border

---

4. O'Neill, Bard E. (1990). *Insurgency and Terrorism: Inside Modern Revolutionary Warfare.* Washington DC: Brassey's. p.154.

5. Hosmer, Stephen T. (1990). *The Army's Role in Counterinsurgency and Insurgency.* Santa Monica, CA: RAND. pp.30–1.

6. These military objectives of Operation Enduring Freedom were stated by President George W. Bush in his 20 September 2001 Address to a Joint Session of Congress and his 7 October address to the country. Got details, see "Operation Enduring Freedom – Afghanistan", at <*http://www.globalsecurity.org/military/ops/enduring-freedom.htm*>

7. Barno, David W. (2004). *Afghanistan: The Security Outlook.* Washington DC: Center for Strategic and International Studies.

in Peshawar and Waziristan.[8] The Taliban and foreign jihadis conduct most of their financing and recruiting operations on the Pakistani side of the border.[9] An alliance of Pakistani religious political parties broadly sympathetic to the Taliban, the Muttahida Majlis-e-Amal (MMA), provide support and funding.

US military officials hold that the Taliban's most important leadership council, the Quetta Shura, is based in the capital of Pakistan's Balochistan Province; the important Peshawar Shura is headquartered in NWFP.[10] Gulbuddin Hekmatyar operates in the tribal areas of Dir and Bajur. Jalaluddin Haqqani is based in Waziristan and al-Qaeda has a presence in both Waziristan and Chitral—all Pakistani regions that border Afghanistan.[11] Intelligence reports indicate that Pakistan's Inter-Services Intelligence (ISI) is continuing to actively support the Taliban leadership.[12]

While the top Taliban leaders have found refuge in Pakistani cities, its fighters are ensconced in the Pakistan-Afghanistan border areas. These areas have historically been 'ungoverned spaces' and are inhabited predominantly by the Pashtun tribe, with strong ethno-tribal affiliations to the Taliban. Unlike the traditional insurgencies, the Afghan insurgent today fights to preserve the *status quo* of ungoverned spaces or to repel an occupier; the insurgents are thus mostly "strategically reactive."[13] In this primitive, traditional, xenophobic, underdeveloped Pashtun heartland, local tribes fiercely resist any modernisation campaign and have provided support to the Taliban in

8. Kucera, Joshua (2004). "Counter-Insurgency in Afghanistan: Paving the Way For Peace", *Jane's Defence Weekly*, 9 December.

9. Rashid, Ahmed (2003). "Who's Winning the War on Terror?", *Yale Global*, 5 September.

10. Bergen, Peter (2007). "Afghanistan 2007: Problems, Opportunities and Possible Solutions", House Committee on Foreign Affairs, 15 February, at *<http://foreignaffairs.house.gov/110/ber021507.htm>* (accessed 10 October 2008).

11. Ibid.

12. Rubin, Barnett R. (2007). "Saving Afghanistan", *Foreign Affairs*, Jan.–Feb., at *<http://www.foreignaffairs.org/20070101faessay86105/barnett-r-rubin/saving-afghanistan.html>* (accessed 27 April 2007).

13. Such patterns are readily recognisable in historical examples of resistance warfare, but less so in classical counter-insurgency theory. See Becket, Ian F.W. (1988). *The Roots of Counter-Insurgency: Armies and Guerrilla Warfare 1900–1945*. London: Blandford; Laqueur, Walter (1977). *Guerrilla*. London: Weidenfeld and Nicholson.

accordance with their tribal code of Pashtunwali.[14] Training camps have been organised in the tribal regions of western Pakistan bordering Afghanistan.

There are no good statistics on the numerical strength of the Taliban forces. Data extrapolated from several sources in 2005 suggest that they may possess between 2000 and 4000 full-time fighters.[15] Taliban sources claim a much higher figure. Late Taliban commander Mullah Dadullah, in his interview to *Al Jazeera* in 2006 put Taliban forces at 12,000 fighters—larger than the US estimates of 7000 to 10,000.[16] The rest are part-time fighters, young Afghan men who have been alienated by government corruption or angry at civilian deaths caused by American bombing raids or simply in search of cash.[17]

The foreign jihadi component of the Taliban, estimated to be about 2000 in number,[18] comprise an amalgam of loosely knit extremists, loosely affiliated with al-Qaeda. Most jihadis are from Pakistan, Uzbekistan and Tajikistan; and a minority from Sudan, Egypt, Saudi Arabia, Iraq, Yemen, Somalia, and Chechnya. Afghan and American officials indicate that the foreign fighters could also be coming from Turkey and western China.[19]

Problem Areas

'Ungoverned Spaces' and External Actors

A complex web of international networks of armed groups, connected by opium trafficking, ethnic ties and Islamic fundamentalism link Afghanistan with Kashmir, Chechnya, Tajikistan,

14. Under the code of *Pashtunwali* these tribes provide honour, hospitality and revenge. Interviews in Lahore with Ahmed Rashid (25 February 2005) and Faridulah Khan Wazir (28 February 2007). For the tribal nature of the Afghan insurgency see Lobjakas, Ahto (2007). "Afghanistan: NATO Sees 'Tribal' Nature to Taliban Insurgency", RFERL, 20 July, at <*http://www.rferl.org/featuresarticle/2007/07/88253227-f287-4104-a336-0874c98978c2.html*> (accessed 31 July 2007). Also see Johnson, Thomas H. and M. Chris Mason (2007). "Understanding the Taliban and Insurgency in Afghanistan", *Orbis* 51(1): 20 (Winter).

15. Jones, Seth G. (2006) "Averting Failure in Afghanistan", *Survival* 48(1): 112 (Spring).

16. Bergen, "Afghanistan 2007...", n.12.

17. Rohde, David (2007). "Foreign Fighters of Harsher Bent Bolster Taliban", *New York Times* 30 October, at <*http://www.nytimes.com/2007/10/30/world/asia/30afghan.html?_r=1&oref=slogin*>

18. Bergen, "Afghanistan 2007...", n.12.

19. Rohde, "Foreign Fighters of Harsher Bent...".n.19.

Kyrgyzstan, Uzbekistan, Pakistan, Iran, and Central Asia in an arc of "regional conflict formation".[20]

Inside Afghanistan and its neighbouring countries, economic activities outside formal legal structures are viewed as legitimate by a section of the population. This "grey market" exploits the lack of governmental control in border areas, provides funds to regional warlords through illegal taxes, corruption of government officials, promoting an atmosphere of continuing instability throughout the country. More importantly, it provides funding and recruitment for the Taliban–al-Qaeda insurgency. Coupled with covert state support for armed groups, this region is emerging as the hub of instability and violence, and haven for the Taliban–al-Qaeda combine.

Cross-border social and ethnic ties connect these destabilising networks and undermine the government's efforts to bring stability. In addition to the history of Taliban support in this "ungoverned" area among the ethnic Pashtun, this is one of the most underdeveloped regions of the world. The Durand Line, which forms the Afghanistan–Pakistan border, "has fostered emigration, smuggling, drug trafficking, and recruitment to militant groups in territories where the Pakistani and Afghan states have been unwilling or unable to maintain firm control."[21] The Taliban–al-Qaeda have complete freedom of movement, and often seek refuge in their havens in Pakistan.

While the US-led forces with their intrusive search operations and aerial bombings are causing collateral damage and resentment among the local populace, the Taliban are fighting a classic "war of the flea",[22] largely along lines used against the Soviet army by the mujahideen, including hiding and fighting in villages to deliberately provoke air strikes. The lack of understanding of the geographic and ethnographic terrain among the international forces is working to their advantage. The insurgent by using high levels of violence aims to provoke the government to over-react with use of force that would cause "collateral damage", further reducing its moral legitimacy and credibility among

20. See Rubin, Barnett R. and Andrea Armstrong (2003). "Regional Issues in the Reconstruction of Afghanistan", *World Policy Journal*, Spring.

21. Ibid.

22. See Taber, Robert (2002). *War of the Flea: The Classic Study of Guerrilla Warfare*. Washington DC: Potomac.

the people. These small acts by the insurgents gradually increase in scope, until the population reaches a "tipping point". Unless the government exhibits its capacity to thwart these attacks and provide protection for the population, it runs the risk of losing its "moral legitimacy" and support from the people.

Taliban tactics and operations against the coalition forces are gaining in strength and lethality. The Taliban have published their first military field manual, which is similar in its objectives to British and American military field manuals, detailing how to spring ambushes, run spies, and conduct an insurgency against the coalition forces.[23] In 2006-07, apart from traditional open engagement with Afghan and international forces, the Taliban continued "asymmetric warfare" in the form of roadside and suicide bombings, primarily targeting Afghan security forces, government officials, and international troops.

The booming drug trade is a source of revenue for the warlords, insurgents and criminal organisations in control of Afghanistan's border regions, as well as for members of the government.[24] The cultivation of opium poppy has markedly increased since Operation Enduring Freedom. The income of Afghan opium farmers and traffickers is equivalent to roughly 40 per cent of the country's GDP, which includes both licit and illicit activity. According to a US military official, charities and individual donations from the Middle East also boost the Taliban's coffers. These twin revenue streams—drug money and Middle East contributions—allow the Taliban to pay their fighters $100 or more a month, which compares favourably to the $70 salary of an Afghan police officer.[25]

Afghan National Army

While the conventional approach adopted by the US forces has not

---

23. The Taliban military manual is divided into 10 chapters of 144 pages and appears to be the result of collaboration between religious scholars and specialists in terrorist, logistical and intelligence tactics. It is illustrated with simple formulas for the preparation of explosives, pictures and diagrams of light and heavy weaponry, ammunition and communication equipment. See Wilkinson, Isambard and Ashraf Ali (2007). "How to be a Jihadi: Taliban's Training Secrets", *The Telegraph*, 20 August, at <*http://www.telegraph.co.uk/news/main.jhtml?xml=/news/2007/08/16/wtaliban116.xml*> (accessed 22 August 2007).

24. Rubin, Barnett R. (2004). *Road to Ruin: Afghanistan's Booming Opium Industry*. New York: Center on International Cooperation.

25. Bergen, "Afghanistan 2007...", n.12.

proved beneficial in counter-insurgency (COIN), building up of the primary indigenous internal security force in Afghanistan, the ANA could have been a viable alternative for COIN operations in that country. ANA was initially organised, trained, and equipped by the USSF in 2002[26] and later the US Army National Guard soldiers from Task Force Phoenix along the "conventional" US light infantry models. However, the ANA modelled in the image of a conventional army has been primarily employed to augment the coalition's conventional COIN forces rather than augmenting its independent role. ANA training and mission, encompassing the conventional COIN tactics to include "presence patrols" and movement-to-contact (i.e., "clear and sweep") operations, have continuously proven ineffective for providing long-term stability in COIN conflicts.[27]

Also, the ANA has not met its target level strength of 70,000. There have been personnel problems associated with ethnic representation. At the time of the ANA's establishment the Northern Alliance leaders dominated the recruitment toward the Tajik ethnic base, alienating the Pashtuns who shunned recruitment to the ANA. The problem has been partly alleviated with better pay packages as also the appointment of additional Pashtuns in senior Defence Ministry positions.[28]

Afghan National Police

The core component of any COIN force is a well-trained and effective police responsible for security and intelligence collection at the community level. The US and Germany are training the Afghan National Police (ANP) force. Like the ANA, the ANP too has been saddled with problems of funding, training, recruitment, and equipment. It remains under-trained, under-manned, has minimal control in the urban centres, and almost no presence or control over the villages, where it is needed the most. The police work in their communities, often embroiling them

26. "Global Security, Afghanistan—Army", at <*http://www.globalsecurity.org/military/world/afghanistan/army.htm* (accessed 10 February 2008).

27. The US Army appears to be repeating its similar mistake during its Vietnam engagement, when it trained the South Vietnamese Army (ARVN) in its own "conventional" image. See Krepinevich Jr., Andrew F. (1986). *The Army and Vietnam*. Maryland: John Hopkins University Press, pp.22–3.

28. Gall, Carlotta (2003). "In a Remote Corner, an Afghan Army Evolves from Fantasy to Slightly Ragged Reality", *New York Times*, 25 January.

in local factional or ethnic disputes and continuing interference from local warlords. The strength of ANP works out to a ratio of approximately 180 police per 100,000 inhabitants; in the United States the ratio is 244, and in Germany, 292.[29]

Provincial Reconstruction Teams

The provincial reconstruction teams (PRTs) are an innovative approach to resolve the "security–reconstruction" dilemma in Afghanistan. PRTs were created by the US Department of Defense as a platform to provide secure areas for international aid workers beyond the capital in December 2002. As of date, the number of PRTs is 25 with five regional command centres. PRT activities range from resolving local disputes to coordinating local reconstruction projects, although the US-led PRTs focus mainly on counter-insurgency in Southern Afghanistan.

Described as the "leading edge" of the allies' effort to stabilise Afghanistan, the PRTs are integrated civilian-military organisations designed to meet three objectives: improve security, extend the reach of the government, and facilitate reconstruction in priority provinces.[30] With the objective of maintaining light international security "footprint" and building the capacity of Afghan institutions to address instability in remote, ungoverned regions, PRTs were established in 2002.[31]

The PRTs are intended to build trust among the people by participating in the reconstruction of the country and providing a permanent presence, and thereby security. By this principle of classic counter-insurgency—protecting the population from the guerrillas and winning the support of the population in one limited area—the teams can deprive insurgents of that support. However, there are significant problems limiting the performance of the PRTs. For instance, "national caveats" create problems of coordination between and among the PRTs. Most allies with high risk aversion are hesitant to actively engage with

29. United Nations Office on Drugs and Crime (2000). *Seventh United Nations Survey on Crime Trends and the Operations of Criminal Justice Systems, 1998–2000.*

30. Briefing on the role of PRT at ISAF HQ, Kabul, 17 June 2007. Also see ISAF PRT Handbook, Edition 3, 3 February 2007.

31. The PRTs were established at the end of 2002. For detailed information on PRT, see Katzman, Kenneth (n.d.). "Afghanistan: Post-War Governance, Security and U.S. Policy", *Congressional Research Service (CRS) Report* RL30588.

the Afghan population. With little or no oversight of how their funds are managed and projects implemented, PRT projects are stymied by corruption and delays, and are viewed as a "mixed bag". While the performance of the PRTs was plagued, particularly early in their existence, by a lack of funds, expertise, training and poor long-term planning of development projects, currently major criticisms have been levelled against the PRTs for weak inter-agency cooperation, and the relationship between their military and civilian personnel in terms of cooperation and leadership.

The PRTs have been criticised by the NGO community for three reasons. First, they replicate the work of NGOs, blurring the lines between military and development work, placing them in danger as insurgents see the NGOs as partisan. Also, there is a concern that the PRTs "have neither the capacity nor the intent to confront the countrywide security threats now facing the Afghan people and are last to help in times of crisis".[32] The lack of personnel mostly affects the ability of the PRTs to spread beyond the towns in which they are located. Counter-insurgency theory calls for an "inkblot" strategy, wherein the stability created by counter-insurgents in one area can gradually spread to other areas. The small number of PRTs and the limited number of personnel attached to them (rarely more than 150) means that there is a limitation on the capability of US and coalition forces to reach beyond the immediate confines of the existing PRTs.[33]

Disarmament, Demobilisation, and Reintegration (DDR) and Disarmament of Illegal Armed Groups (DIAG) Programme

The Disarmament, Demobilisation, and Reintegration (DDR) programme administered by the United Nations Assistance Mission for Afghanistan (UNAMA) to dismantle illegal militias and curb regionalism. This programme got off to a slow start because the Afghan Defence Ministry did not enact mandated reforms (primarily reduction of the number of Tajiks in senior positions) by the targeted 1 July 2003 date. The DDR programme had initially been expected to

32. This was stated by an Afghan NGO Security official in Mazar-e-Sharif, 6 June 2007. Discussions with NGO personnel in different provinces of Afghanistan in June 2007 also highlighted similar thinking.

33. This inference has been drawn from briefings and discussions with Afghan government officials and Afghans in Kabul, June 2007.

demobilise 100,000 fighters, although that figure was later dropped to just over 60,000 by Afghan officials.

Critics of the demobilisation programme call it a "bad joke" as the promised "vocational retraining programmes" are virtually non-existent, and the militias have retained most of their weapons and many are back to the old ways. There has been mounting criticism of the DDR programme for failing to prevent rearmament of militiamen or stockpiling of weapons and for rehiring some militiamen in programmes run by the US and its partners.[34] The government attempts to neutralise the growing influence of the warlords by assimilating them into the new government as provincial governors or ministers. This move has invited wide criticism for advancing the "culture of impunity".

Compromised Security

Security in Afghanistan is being undermined by inadequate COIN efforts to grapple with the interrelated threats posed by the powerful warlords, militias, and massive drug trade as well as the inadequacies of Security Sector Reform.[35] Rather than marginalising the warlords and dismantling their militias, the US, in numerous cases, has relied upon the warlords for intelligence and cooperation in efforts to nab the Taliban–al-Qaeda remnants.[36] The absence of adequate number of troops and sufficient resources has in part contributed to the government's failure to secure the countryside. The number of troops and financial assistance has been among the lowest of any stability operation since World War II.

Even the limited number of US forces was too focused on offensive "clear and sweep" operations against al-Qaeda–Taliban and rarely sought to hold land, occupy villages and towns, or cultivate relations with the locals. Instead, to combat the insurgency these forces launched a number of search operations, sending ground forces into

34. For details of the DDR programme, see Dennys, Christian (2005). "Disarmament, Demobilization and Rearmament?", 6 June, at <*http://www.jca.apc.org/~jann/Documents/Disarmament%20 demobilization%20rearmament.pdf*> (accessed 1 February 2008).

35. Sedra, Mark (2006). "Security Sector Reform in Afghanistan: The Slide Towards Expediency", *International Peacekeeping* 13(1) 94–110 (March).

36. Rupp, Richard (2006). "High Hopes and Limited Prospects: Washington's Security and Nation-Building Aims in Afghanistan", *Cambridge Review of International Affairs* 19(2): 291 (June).

an area supported by air power. The resulting collateral damage and mounting civilian deaths further antagonised the population. The search operations were aggressive and were seen as violating the religious and cultural rights of the people.[37] Increasingly, American forces are being viewed as an "occupying force" and anti-American sentiment runs high among the populace.[38]

Inadequate Economic Assistance

An essential COIN goal remains separating the populace from the warlords, drug lords and insurgents, and giving them a viable economic choice. In Afghanistan, despite huge international pledges of financial grants and loans, the goal of rebuilding a stable country remains distant. According to United Nations and World Bank data, post-Taliban Afghanistan continues to trail at the bottom of every economic indicator list.[39]

In the early years of the COIN operations (2001-2003) in Afghanistan, the US government depicted an aversion to nation-building and maintained a light security footprint[40] with low levels of economic assistance.[41] A 2006 US Government Accountability Office (GAO) report calculated that for the 2004 budget year, the US was "contributing about 38 per cent of the $3.6 billion pledged by the international community".[42] The US government has appropriated $27 billion for Iraqi reconstruction but only $7 billion for Afghanistan—a country that is roughly the same size in population, a third larger geographically, and utterly destroyed by two decades of war. Of the

37. Discussions with former Afghan Minister Ali A. Jalali, Washington DC, October 2005. Also see Jalali, A.A. (2003). "Afghanistan in 2002", *Asian Survey* 43(1): 174–85.

38. This observation was arrived at by "person on the street" narratives in various provinces of Afghanistan during the field visit in May–June 2007.

39. With life expectancy at 46.4 years, GDP per capita of just $315, 70 per cent of the population below the poverty line and official unemployment rate at a conservative 30 per cent.

40. Interview with Ambassador James Dobbins, RAND, Washington DC, 9 September 2005.

41. The United States committed some $500 million in reconstruction aid to Afghanistan in 2001, in direct comparison of $18 billion in economic assistance the Bush Administration requested in 2003 for Iraq, a country of comparable size, much greater wealth, and much less damaged.

42. Considering Afghanistan's staggering needs, the expenditure by the US government of $1.4 billion during this crucial period seems limited in light of the monthly expenditure of $1 billion to fund the American military presence in the country. See Rupp, "High Hopes and Limited Prospects...". n.38.

money appropriated, a State Department official has conveyed that only $2.5 billion has actually been spent, despite Afghanistan's larger land mass and greater infrastructure needs.[43] That works out to a paltry $20 per year per Afghan over the past five years. Without greater investments in roads, access to water and employment opportunities, the Taliban prosper and continue to gain adherents.

The huge gap between short-term high-visibility projects, which heightens people's expectations, without any follow-up action in terms of job creation or building an indigenous industrial base, is fuelling discontent among the local populace, and thereby providing a support base for the Taliban. There is a need to build the local indigenous agricultural and industrial base for employment generation, and the development of a sustainable economy. Else, Afghanistan a 'rentier state' would continue to depend on outside aid for decades to come.[44]

NATO's Conflicting Agenda

In addition, the effectiveness of NATO's participation in Afghanistan COIN campaign is hampered by the following constraints:

The problem of resources and troop contribution of some NATO members to provide troops for the Afghan mission is "undermining NATO's credibility" and its operations.[45] In the face of rising violence and increasing lethality of attacks from Taliban-led insurgency, NATO officials have repeatedly explored the possibility of shifting forces from other parts of Afghanistan but "national caveats" placed on how and where a country's military forces may be employed limit flexibility in conducting combat operations, thereby creating operational constraints. The "national caveats" (national restrictions) imposed by NATO allies on their forces in Afghanistan include "geographical restrictions on locations of units deployments as well as nature of missions units are allowed to participate and are intended to restrict the affected units from participating in offensive combat operations or other operations that

43. Bergen, "Afghanistan 2007...", n.12.

44. D'Souza, Shanthie Mariet (2007). "Change the Pattern of Aid to Afghanistan", IDSA Strategic comments, 28 June, at <*http://idsa.in/publications/stratcomments/ShanthieDSouza280607.htm*> (accessed 10 August 2008).

45. Interview with Ambassador Karl Inderfurth, Washington DC, 16 February 2006. Also see Inderfurth, Karl F. (2007). "A Last Chance", *The Boston Globe*, 8 August, at <*http://www.iht.com/articles/2007/08/08/opinion/edinder.php*> (accessed 10 August 2007)

carry a high risk of casualties".[46] This risk avoidance and risk aversion[47] undermines the effectiveness of the NATO forces.

There is also the *problem of unity of command* and *conflicting national agendas*. The attempt to merge the ISAF and OEF under one command has been resisted by the NATO allies mainly because of differing perceptions on the nature of the two operations and conflicting national agendas. While Britain and Germany wished to preserve ISAF as stabilisation as opposed to combat mission, Britain, leading the ISAF counter-narcotics effort intended to retain the initiative in the political sphere. While the US counter narcotics policy centred on use force like aerial spraying, the British believe that using force against Afghan poppy cultivators to eradicate the poppy crop might result in losing the hearts-and-minds campaign and broadening the support base of the insurgency.[48] In Helmand province, for instance, rural communities, in addition to turning anti-government, look to the insurgents for "protection" of poppy crops. In other provinces, the alternative crop seeds provided to farmers were either highly unsuitable to climatic conditions or have not been sustainable.

Is there an Alternative Strategy?

In establishing linkages between development and security, the inkblot strategy employed successfully by the British in Malaya 50 years ago, involves focusing military effort not on hunting down the enemy but instead securing key centres and improving conditions to eliminate support for an insurgency, with success then spreading slowly outward

---

46. Feickert, Andrew (2006). "US and Coalition Military Operations in Afghanistan: Issues for Congress", *CRS Report* RL33503, updated 11 December.

47. Mills, Greg (2007). "Ten Counterinsurgency Commandments from Afghanistan", Foreign Policy Research Institute, April, at <*http://www.fpri.org/enotes/200704.mills.afghanistancounter insurgency.html*> (accessed 28 June 2007).

48. Germany opposed a merger of the commands because German forces in ISAF were trained only for stabilisation, and not for counter-insurgency operations. The French view was somewhat different; they were concerned that the Administration, after having a US commander in place to guide all military activity in Afghanistan, might use NATO as a "toolbox" to accomplish Washington's broader objectives. See Gallis, Paul (2007). "NATO in Afghanistan: A Test of the Transatlantic Alliance", Congressional Research Service Report, RL33627, updated 16 July. Also see Dempsey, Judy and David S. Cloud (2005). "Europeans balking at new Afghan role", 14 September, at <*http://www.iht.com/articles/2005/09/13/news/nato.php*> (accessed 1 July 2007).

as if from an expanding ink spot.[49] The need is to extend governance and prosperity through "ink spots" of relative stability, employing unity of effort by nations and institutions.[50]

An important step forward would be the "Clear, Hold, Build and Engage"[51] strategy—clear the area from the enemy, hold the territory, build infrastructure and resources, and engage with the local community. The success of this approach will depend on ensuring better coordination and faster delivery among international and local actors, realising political and capacity constraints, and, ultimately, enabling the Afghan government to take responsibility and control on its own terms. This strategy demands focus of effort and consolidation of gains, without which the insurgent "balloon" will simply distort and not deflate as intended.[52] This strategy would help build up the local forces and support in ensuring long-term stability and development.

An alternative and durable course of action would be to recast the COIN strategy with indigenous Afghan forces playing a crucial role. The "unconventional COIN campaign model" proposes a shift away from the conventional strategy to include Constabulary Force (CF), village Self-Defence Force (SDF), Movement-to-Contact Force (MTC), and Quick Reaction Force (QRF) with the US Army Special Forces (USSF) playing an advisory role to the Afghan CF. The unconventional warfare campaign model focuses on population control instead of "clear and sweep operations". While the COIN approach has focused narrowly on instant quick-fix method, the larger goal of institution-building and building the Afghan state's capacity to deal with its internal problems seems to be missing.

Successful COIN responses by foreign forces require a detailed understanding of the population's culture and sensitising the forces towards local customs. An effective COIN strategy envisions meeting

---

49. Mills, Greg Terrence McNamee and Denny Lane (2006). "Security Vortex, Warlords and Nation Building", *The National Interest*, 9 January, at <*http://www.nationalinterest.org/Article.aspx?id=11952*> (accessed 15 May 2007).

50. In Afghanistan, during the tenure of the ninth International Security Assistance Force (ISAF IX) deployed between May 2006 and February 2007, this evolved into Afghan Development Zones (ADZs), providing a focus of development spending and security effort. Mills, Greg. "Ten Counterinsurgency Commandments...", n.49.

51. Ibid.

52. Gall, Carlotta (2007). "British Make Initial Gains Against Taliban", *New York Times*, 5 August.

the citizen's needs in order to regain the moral legitimacy and isolate the insurgents. It is important to counter the growing Taliban influence by reconstruction and development projects particularly in the villages in the south and provinces bordering with Pakistan's tribal areas. An effective counter-narcotics approach needs to be buttressed by an alternative livelihood programme for the poor farmers. Demobilised militia need to be given adequate vocational training or recruited for COIN purposes rather than letting them be utilised as recruiting material by the Taliban–al-Qaeda forces.

While the inability of US forces to counter the rising levels of attacks would lead to legitimacy problems for the Afghan government, an effective course of action would be to strengthen the Afghan face of the COIN. The current Afghan war will be won or lost within the villages, especially those on the volatile Afghan–Pakistan frontier and "ungoverned spaces". Thus, "main effort" indigenous COIN force must have access to the social networks within these villages. This could come from the Afghan Constabulary Force that is primarily recruited from the local population, lives in the local population, operates in the community on a daily basis, and provides security for the local population with easy access to the grassroots level social networks for effective intelligence collection.

Though the raging insurgency might not be able to topple the Karzai government, popular discontent at the slow pace of reconstruction and lack of security could tilt the people's support towards the insurgents. In Afghanistan no one ever took national power by fighting decisive battles but by gaining people's support. It seems likely that the 'tipping point' is reached. The need for the international community to coordinate its efforts, and strengthen the Afghan ownership and participation in rebuilding the country is crucial. Else, the international effort would resemble a foreign project that the Afghans could ultimately reject. There is also a need for a regional strategy to effectively deal with the problem of sanctuary and enhance the participation of regional countries in building a stable Afghanistan.

8

Post-Taliban Afghanistan

Conflict, Violence and Regional Stability

ANUP KUMAR DATTA

If the international forces leave, the Taliban will take over in one hour.
—Afghan cabinet member, September 2006

The successive wars have ruined Afghanistan's state-building process. Between 1.5 million and 2 million Afghans have died in the wars; 5 to 6 million have fled to neighbouring Pakistan and Iran; hundreds of thousands have died in famines, poverty, intra-community conflicts, and the warlords' race for supremacy. The recent history of Afghanistan witnessed a vast array of conflicts between a Soviet-backed Marxist regime and nascent Islamic resistance movements (1978–79), Soviet Red Army and potential armed resistance of the mujahideen guerrillas (1979–1989), factional conflicts between Afghans (1989–1996), followed by the emergent Taliban forces and Northern opposition forces (1996–2001), until the US-led coalition removed the Taliban in 2001 November.[1] This chapter seeks to analyse the character of the Afghan conflict. The first section analyses the nature and the dynamics of the present crisis. The second section focuses on the role of the opium economy and its linkages with terrorism. The third section examines the role played by the regional actors and the nature of the US engagement and that of the coalition. The concluding part discusses the future directions of Afghanistan and prospects for its stability.

Dynamics of the Crisis

Developments after ousting the Taliban regime in 2001 have not

1. Hagerty, Devin and H. Hagerty (2006). "The Reconstitution and Reconstruction of Afghanistan", in Devin Hagerty (ed.), *South Asia in World Politics*. Oxford University Press.

augured well for state building, reconstruction, and development in Afghanistan. The exponential rise of insurgency—the proliferation of improvised explosive devices (IEDs) and the spiralling role of suicide bombing, the hesitancy and confusion in the US-led coalition forces, the lack of reconstruction efforts and want of political will—have been accompanied by a huge spurt of drug and weapon trafficking.[2] What passes for governance today is the dominance of regional warlords and informal/illicit economy. Afghanistan is witnessing a classical counter-insurgency where "the centre of gravity in a conflict is the people". The Afghan citizen is dissatisfied in all areas of basic concern—security, governance, rule of law, human rights, unemployment and poverty, lack of sustainable economic welfare, and lack of participation in the decentralisation process.[3] Afghanistan has been infected with the so-called Dutch disease—large inflows of drug proceeds, aid and remittances, a high-cost, high-risk economy for investment, low employment, and low growth in the formal sector.[4]

Five Ps sum up the present Afghan dilemma—poverty, politics, poppy, Pakistan, and patron-clientelism. Poverty is widespread. So is the internal politics of the warlords. These are linked to the booming poppy cultivation and the drug economy, which generates huge cash resources and which allow the Taliban to pay their fighters $100 or more a month, compared to $70 an Afghan police officer earns. Pakistan is the nucleus of the global reach of terrorists. Pakistan's ISI (Inter-Services Intelligence) continues to patronise the Taliban leadership operating near Baluchistan. Pakistan-based Taliban insurgents have been vigorously extending their presence in the southern and eastern parts of Afghanistan.[5] More than 925 Afghan policemen have died in Taliban ambushes. Today it is difficult to travel between Kabul and Kandahar because of the Taliban influence in nearly half of the districts of Ghazni province.

Why is it that after so much effort by the coalition forces and the Northern Alliance, the situation remains so grave? The answer may be

2. See The Report of the Secretary General (2007). "The Situation in Afghanistan and its Implications for International Peace and Security", 21 September.

3. Barnett, R. Rubin (2007). "Saving Afghanistan", *Foreign Affairs* 86(1) (Jan./Feb.).

4. Afghanistan in 2007; A survey report.

5. The SENLIS Council report (2007). "Stumbling into Chaos". November.

found in mistakes both by the US administration and neglect of the real crisis in Afghanistan—the crisis of legitimacy confronted by the Karzai government. Regionalism and warlordism are the realities of Afghan history. The United States, Pakistan, and Saudi Arabia poured in billions of dollars initially to back the anti-communist Afghan mujahideen and their Arab auxiliaries, creating a permanent infrastructure of regional and global jihad. In the 1990s, with the collapse of the Soviet State, drug trafficking boomed and the jihadis strengthened their bases. With Pakistan's assistance, the Taliban established control over most of Afghanistan. Afghanistan's rising drug trade was able to expand the base of Taliban ranks. Additional sources of funds were remittances from the Middle East. Notwithstanding the Taliban's decree on 27 July 2000 banning opium cultivation, Afghanistan's opium still accounted for 75 per cent of the world's supply.[6]

The resurgence of the Taliban is closely connected to Pakistan. The Taliban's leadership council, the Quetta Shura, is situated in Pakistan's Baluchistan province; the Peshawar Shura is headquartered in the North-West Frontier Province (NWFP). Jalaluddin Haqqani is based in Waziristan and al-Qaeda exists in Waziristan and Chitral in Pakistan.[7] An alliance of Pakistani religious political parties sympathetic to the Taliban, the Muttahida Majlis-e-Amal (MMA) controls both the NWFP and Baluchistan.

The resurgence of the Taliban is also rooted in the failures of the Karzai government to ensure security, rule of law, and reconstruction. The head of the Ulema Council of Kandahar noted that "the Taliban are from the people". The government and the international community have failed to provide basic services, security, and employment to the rural communities. Lack of an effective police force and corruption among the police and the Afghan National Army (ANA) have created a state within the state. The Afghan Human Rights Commission notes that more than 80 per cent of the winning candidates in the provinces and 60 per cent in Kabul in the 2004 elections maintained strong alliances with the armed groups. A former

6. *Annual Opium Survey in Afghanistan, 2007.*
7. Special Report, USIS, 162, June 2006.

Taliban governor, Mantri Mohammed Islam Mohammadi, who was a witness in the destruction of the Buddha statues in Bamiyan, won the 2004 elections. The Lower House of Paliament, *Wolesi Jirga*, is composed of the Islamists and mujahideen, including four former Taliban commanders—they won at least half of the 249 seats. The government's accommodative approach to pull together the warlords, the drug dealers, the tribal leaders, and a distinct variety of power-brokers has led to the breakdown of governance.[8] While the people in general resent Talibanism and insurgency or violation of gender rights they equally resent their ostracisation from the process of democratic participation and institution-building, and lack of a consistent rule of law. One hawker complained, "The Taliban beat us and ask for food, and then the government beats us for helping the Taliban." Many in Afghanistan say that the police are the main criminals.[9]

The Opium Economy

The illicit cultivation of poppy and drug trafficking constitutes the crux of corruption, violence, and warlordism in Afghanistan. Currently, the country produces 93 per cent of the world's illegal opium output. The drug economy generates $3 billion annually, most of which flows out of the country and the farmers get only $600 million. Three million Afghans are virtually dependent on opium production and trafficking. The international community's counter-strategy to contain opium production has failed—neither the eradication programme nor aerial spraying and manual destruction has helped. The opium farmers have no alternative livelihoods.[10] The insurgents and the warlords gain financially from drug convoys and taxing drugs, and promoting an illicit economy beyond government control. The World Bank documents that the drug economy is centred round a few powerful and well-connected actors, which ensures the traffickers' protection and enriches the coffers of the wealthier opium producers. Ahmed Ali Karzai, the younger brother of President Karzai, and currently the head

8. Sherman, Jake (2005). "Disarming Afghanistan's Warlords", *Fletcher Journal of Human Security* XX.
9. *Foreign Affairs*, 86(1) (January/February 2007).
10. Ham, Peter and J. Kaminga (2006/07). "Poppies for Peace: Reforming Afghanistan's Opium Industry", *Washington Quarterly* (Winter).

of the Provincial Council of Kandahar, is allegedly having a big share of the drugs trade. The dominance of the opium economy forces any elite family to have a connection with it.[11] The drug mafia make use of both the formal and informal channels of the government, and the Taliban. The Taliban maintains a corporate identity as an umbrella for militant Islamists, drug barrons, tribal elders, and warlords. Al-Qaeda uses the profits from opium trade to support and maintain its terrorist network in Iraq, Burma (Myanmar), Afghanistan, and Latin America. In 2004, the US Drug Enforcement Agency set up a Central Poppy Eradication Force and urged the locals to abandon poppy cultivation in favour of production of cotton, nuts, and fruits. The proposal was vehemently resented. In 2006, opium production was 6100 tonnes, an increase of 49 per cent over 2005.[12] The number of persons involved in opium cultivation in 2006 was 2.9 million; in 2007 it grew to 3.3 million, which constitutes 14.3 per cent of the population.[13] The SENLIS Council suggested that instead of eradication, burning and spraying of chemicals, Afghanistan can capitalise effectively on the expertise of the farmers by diverting part of the existing illegal opium to the domestic and global market.[14] Opium licensing presents an economically viable alternative to production of WHO-prescribed medicines, morphine and codeine. This would integrate the dissidents into the legal economy, expand the government's tax base, and help to curtail terrorism and transnational crime.

Most of the poppy cultivated in 2007 was in Helmand, Kandahar, Uruzgan, Day Kundi, Farah, and Nimroz provinces, where the security situation is abysmal. The major customs posts of Herat, Kandahar and Jalalabad which produce considerable revenues are under the insurgents' control.[15] Many members of the police/army are involved in the sale of commissions, postings, and other forms of corruption. A strong nexus exists between the warlords, police, smugglers and the Taliban, which also provides regional-level constellations against the

11. Schetter, Conrad and Others (2007). "Beyond Warlordism: The Local Security Architecture in Afghanistan", IPG 2.
12. *Annual Opium Survey, 2007.*
13. Ibid.
14. Ham and Kaminga, "Poppies for Peace ...", n.10.
15. *Regional Studies* (Islamabad), Vol. 1 (Winter 2006-07).

state. The vicious cycle exists because in Afghanistan, the state is weak at the base and heavy at the top. The appointment of the tribal notables rather than proven administrators as governors obstructs the process of good governance.[16] Perhaps, the disease or virus of narcotics constitutes a bigger development and security issue today than earlier.[17]

Regional Actors and International Intervention

Afghanistan was always considered a buffer state and the USA, Britain, Iran, China, India, and Pakistan shared often symmetrical and mostly divergent approaches in steering their policies towards Afghanistan. Iran's policy towards Afghanistan is well orchestrated and multi-angled. It resented the Bonn Agreement and the Afghan Compact. It is strongly against the Taliban's resurgence because they are anti-Shiite. It may be recalled that 11 Iranian diplomats were executed in Mazar-i-Sharif in 1998 by the Taliban government. The antipathy to the Taliban in Iran is also on account of strong nationalism and ideological differences. For Iran, a secure and stable regime in Afghanistan is an ideal situation. Iran is also interested that the refugees from Afghanistan are settled as early as possible. Iran's longstanding security needs depend upon a stable Asia, and shifting and preventing the US encroachment in South Asia.

For the US and the coalition partners, Afghanistan and Iraq are test cases of their foreign policy. The coalition forces are smarting with internal contradictions. Misjudgement and divergent security interests, cut off from the ground reality also account for their failure.[18] The presence of an outsider force is passionately resented in Afghanistan. The conflict there is generated and sustained both by conservatism of the Taliban and Islamic fundamentalism. As long as fundamentalism predominates in Islam, it will be difficult to isolate and support secular, democratic-minded Islam. The Western policy also fails on account of its inability to evolve a comprehensive strategy of

16. About the crisis of governance see the World Bank document, July 2007, "Service Delivery and Governance at the Sub-national Level in Afghanistan".

17. INCSR, 2007, vol. 2.

18. Noetzel, Timo and S. Scheipers (2007). "Coalition Warfare in Afghanistan", *Washington Post*, October.

reconstruction, stability and development, and counter-insurgency operations.

The "war on terror" cannot be won by military means only; it requires a long-term strategy to root out the causes of terror, poverty, and insurgency from the Afghan soil. A country which is ethnically divided, socially fragmented, and politically naïve requires a high level of solidarity and stability to ensure a durable state and democracy. The war in Afghanistan is multi-faceted. It involves the political task of consolidation and legitimating of a fragile state into the democratic framework. Equally, it is an issue of reconstruction, and ensuring human security and welfare for one of the poorest states of the world. Afghanistan is in the limelight and is the nucleus of conflict today because the US and Britain have pursued a wrong Afghanistan policy for a long time. It is not only Afghanistan but also Pakistan which poses the gravest threat to democratic culture in South Asia, as was witnessed in Benazir Bhutto's assassination and the series of bomb blasts in Pakistan, Afghanistan, and India in the last three years. Apart from increasing civil-military cooperation, the idea ought to be one of ensuring security, bringing about law and order, and ensuring welfare to stabilise Afghanistan. If NATO's engagement falters, Afghanistan may again be in chaos.[19]

The Bonn process, which created the country's elected bodies and which was endorsed at the London conference (31 January–1 February 2006) identified the critical areas as security; governance, rule of law and human rights; and social and economic development. The main objective of the Bonn Agreement was to end "the tragic conflict in Afghanistan and promote national reconciliation, lasting peace, stability and human rights in the country". However, the Bonn process was essentially weak, since only a section of the Afghans participated in it.[20] As no political parties participated, the process of robust democratisation could not be initiated.

While the commitment for the reconstruction of Afghanistan was staggering, only 44 per cent of the aid could be used. Notwithstanding the massive aid commitment, the lack of coherence among the

19. SENLIS report (2007). "Stumbling into Chaos". November.

20. ICG report (2007). "Afghanistan's Endangered Compact", 29 January.

coalition members has diluted the anti-insurgency campaign. At the operational level, varying national legal systems for military operations are the biggest constraints. In addition, the "light footprint" approach has led to scarcity of resources. An integrated strategy for combat operations which should mix operations, stability, and reconstruction is also lacking.[21] As a result, the conflict becomes highly asymmetrical. As one Taliban commander commented, "Taking cities is not part of our present tactics. Our tactics are now hit and run...we kill the enemies of Allah there, and retreat to our safe bases in the mountains."

The collapse of the Soviet Union and the emergence of lesser actors like Kyrgyzstan and Tajikistan has made them more vulnerable in the matrix of the Asian security system. All the states bordering Afghanistan are confronted with the proliferation of drugs and small weapons, and possible ingress of refugees from Afghanistan. The Central Asian states are constantly vulnerable to Islamic extremism and Wahabi ideology.

The rise of Talibanism as an ideology of separatism and fundamentalist convictions has also given Pakistan additional influence in Asia.[22] At the same time, since the border areas are porous and Pakistan has a substantial domination of the Pashtun and al-Qaeda in the NWFP and Baluchistan, an unstable Afghanistan is a constant security threat to Pakistan's stability. Intelligence reports confirm that Pakistan's ISI provides strong support to the Taliban and Pakistan's Tribal Agencies of North and South Waziristan are strongly integrated with Taliban fighters and jihadis.[23] A report lists 55 training camps for jihadis all over Pakistan, with 29 located in Pakistan-Occupied Kashmir, 15 in NWFP, 3 in the Northern Areas, 7 in Punjab, and 1 in Sindh.[24] Pakistan's all-out support to the Taliban is guided by both domestic considerations of unity and integrity of the borders with Afghanistan as also to use it as a shield against the dominant Indian influence in Asia in trade and commerce, and to keep the Kashmir issue on the boil.

21. Noetzel and Scheipers, "Coalition Warfare in Afghanistan", n.18.
22. "The Waziristan Accord", *Middle East Review of International Affairs*, December 2007.
23. Ibid.
24. *The Times of India*, 31 July 2005.

In India's perception, the present conflict in Afghanistan is a source of instability and chaos in the region. The basis of democracy in Pakistan being very poor, a failure of democratic state-building and secular Afghanistan would only intensify both border skirmishes and subversion of the process of economic development of South Asia. Escalation of conflict in Afghanistan would erode the prospects of South Asian cooperation and probably dismantle the ethos of democracy and human rights. From a regional and overall global perspective, the existence of unstable regimes poses a severe threat to the burgeoning momentum of institutions. The existence of a crisis state or states would only destabilise the pluralistic, multi-cultural, complex traditions of South Asia.

Prospects

A grand strategy of restoring peace, stability, and reconciliation is imperative for Afghanistan's identity and survival. The grand strategy should combine both security and stability, and ensure the process of democratisation at the centre-peripheral level. The crisis in Afghanistan is fundamentally on account of myriad levels of exploitation and colonial reconstruction. However, in contrast to the Taliban era, Afghanistan is relatively secure: thousands of refugees are returning from Pakistan and Iran, and neighbouring states. According to IMF estimates, the economy is growing, cereal production is up, and macroeconomic management reflects robust growth with only single-digit inflation.[25] While corruption has greatly increased, the management of public finance, telecommunications, education, rise in income, small-scale infrastructure investments, and health care have revived the economy to a significant extent. A lot, however, remains to be done in terms of private sector development, counter-narcotics strategy, reforms and investments in the justice sector, and providing employment to those evicted from poppy cultivation. A few pointers of strategy are given below:

Security

a Track down militant/Islamic extremism in the south/north and contain the forces of transnational terrorism and crime.

25. IMF reports on Afghanistan, 2005–2007.

b Change the opium economy into licit economy.

c Arrest warlordism, and neutralise the dissident and rebel commanders.

d Revamp local security structure.

e Transform the border regions into an arena of cooperation rather than conflict by developing the tribal territories.

f Carry out police/security sector reforms and bring about transparency.

Civic Society

a Ensure human security and development by promoting health, education, and women's rights.

b Reinforce and invigorate civil society institutions.

c Contain pervasive corruption inside and outside the police/army. Ensure human security and welfare of citizens.

d Rehabilitate the refugees with minimum facilities so that they are not allured by the insurgents.

Economic Strategy

a Revive the infrastructure economy, replacing the informal economy.

b Contain unemployment by creation of job opportunities both in the public and the private sectors.

Political Strategy

a The coalition partners should compromise on the divergent security and developmental issues, and build a strong consensus.

b The future of Afghanistan is inevitably linked with the neighbours. India, Pakistan and Iran, apart from the Central Asian states should forge a broader integration and cooperation. They should promote democratic forces to consolidate the state-building process.

c Develop a comprehensive framework of sub-national governance.

d Ensure good governance and sound public delivery system.

e Strengthen the police force and rid it of corrupt practices, by enhancing pay and facilities so that they are not tempted by the warlords and the drug mafia.

f Restore decentralised administration and ensure the democratisation process by offering the warlords a stake in the decision-making process.

g Ensure a transparent judicial system and establish Islamic laws for the whole country.

h Draw up an effective, integrated civilian-military strategy to contain insurgency and weak governance.

i National reconciliation requires dialogue with Pakistan which is virtually a sanctuary of the Taliban elements. The dialogue needs to involve the political forces and local leaders/religious heads.

9

The Problem of Institution Building in Afghanistan

INDRANIL BANERJIE

As we discuss and debate some of the most pressing issues in Asian security and geopolitics, one part of our neighbourhood continues to exist in extreme distress with endemic conflict. It is Afghanistan, turned into a battlefield by conflicting external and internal interests. Afghanistan may be in India's periphery but it is vital to our long-term well-being as conditions there determine the nature of our immediate geopolitical environment. In other words, we can ignore Afghanistan only at our peril.

Over the months and years, we appear to have become inured to the violence and bloodletting in Afghanistan. We have come to assume that the only problem with that country is the egregious Taliban, a force that needs to be annihilated. Our only question seems to be how long will the West hang on in that country. Do NATO and the United States have the will to go on fighting in Afghanistan? Regrettably, these questions obscure some of the more fundamental issues regarding normalisation and stabilisation of Afghanistan. If the objective behind the United States' decision to go into Afghanistan were solely to destroy the Taliban and al-Qaeda, then the Afghan mission is destined to fail. For ideas and ideologies have never been eradicated by the bullet; they have only been defeated by counter-ideologies and opposing notions. In India we have long realised that no insurgency can be defeated by military means alone: the military is only an instrument for creating conditions for political dialogue and processes.

Therefore, the question we must ask of the many players in Afghanistan is whether these activities have aided the creation of political institutions and processes. If the Taliban and its allies are to be defeated, there need to be alternative ideologies and institutions in place that could address the needs of the common Afghan, no matter whether they are Pashtun, Tajik, Hazara, or Aimak. Most fundamentally, there is a pressing requirement for civil institutions that would give ordinary Afghans a greater say in their affairs, in law-making, and resource distribution. There is an equally urgent need for addressing judicial and developmental needs.

Frequent and violent political change in Afghanistan for more than three decades has resulted in the destruction of most institutions of state and civil society. After the US-led military intervention, which led to the ouster of the Taliban regime, it was correctly perceived that Afghanistan could either slide back to anarchy or once again fall prey to a retrogressive regime. The US and its allies therefore, resolved that to stabilise the country and prevent the resurgence of extremist political Islam, it would be necessary to create a progressive, democratic polity. The Bonn Agreement of December 2001 was the first step in this direction. This agreement led to the formation of an interim government. A constitution commission was established to draft a new constitution in consultation with the public. The agreement called for a *loya jirga* and a new constitution was drawn up in 2003. In October 2004, Afghanistan witnessed its first ever presidential elections and Hamid Karzai was elected President. In September 2005, parliamentary polls were held and it seemed that the country was heading in the desired direction.

Unfortunately, despite the right moves at the national level, neither has the parliamentary system taken root nor have democratic institutions of governance. The country is effectively governed through a bureaucracy almost completely controlled by the President's Office. The President also appoints the all-powerful provincial governors, who call the shots outside Kabul. The executive not only remains emasculated but is also considered hugely corrupt. Parliamentarians have little real power except those selected as ministers in the President's cabinet. They complain of their irrelevance in the current set-up. The crucial district elections have been postponed indefinitely and the elected provincial councils have yet to be activated. The village councils, particularly the *jirga*, which was a key part of the traditional Afghan political system, have been excluded from the system.

Ordinary Afghans do not feel that they have a say in governance or policymaking. Resentment is building up at the grassroots.

This chapter looks at the problems of democratisation in Afghanistan and the hindrances to the development of state institutions. It also explores alternative forms of governance that could work in an environment such as Afghanistan. If the current system fails to deliver or remains alien to the country's masses, the US-led coalition will fail to stabilise the country. Without institutions that can take up the space created by the destruction of earlier, and in many cases traditional structures, military action will fail—it will only fuel increasing cycles of conflict and translate into an unending war. This would invariably have a negative fall-out on the whole region in Afghanistan's proximity.

Need for Institution Building

Civil institutions are integral to any modern nation-state and constitute its structural skeleton. Institutions are necessary first, and primarily to solve disputes and resolve conflicts; and also for the formulation and adoption of a common set of rules and laws. Commonly accepted rules, laws, and acceptable practices minimise friction and conflict in a society. Disputes also need to be resolved and rule-breakers or law-breakers meted punishment. The other big role for modern governments is the creation and maintenance of public assets. There is a more historically recent view that state institutions exist to actively aid economic activity and provide utility services like education, health care, public transport, etc. As societies and nations evolve, so does the need for such institutions. Today, for instance, the role of the media is critical in civil society. Then there may be the need to support all kinds of public regulators, ombudsmen and their like to regulate, oversee and guide social, economic, and political activities.

Traditionally, Western political theorists have pointed to the need to establish or have three main pillars for a modern state structure, *viz.*, the legislature, the executive, and the judiciary. An additional postulate is that these three primary institutions need to be independent of each other for the proper functioning of democracy. In feudal times, most often all these functions were carried out by the aristocracy. The king was the lawmaker, arbiter, and administrator rolled into one. Even in colonial India, for instance, the all-powerful district magistrate was in many places both administrator and judge.

In Afghanistan some of the modern state institutions have never existed. The traditional structures that prevented anarchy and served as civil institutions have long been destroyed. Existing informal and formal civil institutions have been corrupted and are unable to provide the average Afghan proper redress, whether political, judicial, or executive. This fundamental hiatus is causing further alienation and increasing the distance between the common Afghan and Kabul.

The judicial system is in shambles. According to a Kabul-based journalist, Wahidullah Amani, the Centre for Policy and Human Development at Kabul University had brought out a report claiming that the state system lagged far behind traditional courts in terms of public confidence and effectiveness. In a questionnaire cited by the report, fewer than 20 per cent of Afghans put the state courts first when asked "Whom do you trust most to resolve any dispute you might have?", while over 70 per cent said that tribal or community elders and *shuras* were their preferred option. The study condemned the state court system for corruption and ineffectiveness, saying that problems in the judiciary were jeopardising the entire structure of governance. The Supreme Court reacted swiftly and decisively, summoning several of the authors for a dressing down. "This report is an absolute lie", said Abdul Rashid Rashed, spokesperson for the Supreme Court. "These people are just against the system. They were summoned to the Supreme Court and questioned about the accuracy of the report, and in the end they accepted that their report was not based on truth. And they apologized."[1]

Even Zalmay Khalilzad, former US envoy to Afghanistan and current US ambassador to the UN, who had operated as something of a king-maker during much of the Karzai regime, while speaking at an American-Afghan business conference in November 2007, remarked: "There is a serious problem of governance in Afghanistan...At the

1. Amani, Wahidullah (2007). "Afghanistan's Creaking Court System", ARR No. 276, December 06, Kabul.

national level, corruption exists at unacceptable levels. At the provincial and district levels, especially in contested areas, government, particularly police, too often is weak, ineffective, sometimes non-existent, and sometimes even predatory". He added that there was "too much polarisation" among Afghan political leaders, a growing opium economy, high unemployment, and lacklustre pace of reconstruction.

Clearly, the existing institutions are not working or are not sufficient. For the average Afghan, especially the rural Pashtuns of southern and eastern parts of the country, Western intervention has hardly changed anything. Rather, things have got worse with military action and air strikes hitting their villages and killing their people. Not surprisingly, the Taliban are creeping back. As soon as troops vacate a town or village, the turbaned Taliban fighters are back. NATO cannot agree to troops' increases and the existing 40,000 soldiers, many of whom do not have a mandate to engage in combat, are simply not enough to hold the ground in even a part of Afghanistan. Worse, the failure to build a political constituency in Afghanistan continues to render the US and NATO forces in the country irrelevant at best, or enemies at worst.

Traditional Governance in Afghanistan

It would be wrong to assume that Afghanistan has been a primitive tribal society or one that has naturally tended towards anarchy. However, it has been a predominantly Pashtun state. Despite existing for many centuries as a loosely federated state, the Pashtuns, after the unification of the country by Ahmad Shah Durrani, who in 1747 founded the monarchy that ruled the country until 1973, were united by the notion of being Afghans and subscribing to certain common traditions and cultural mores. Ahmed Shah was chosen leader of his clan by consensus. He created a vast empire stretching from Punjab in the east to Meshed in the west. Despite Ahmad Shah Durrani's spectacular successes, Kabul's relationship with the provinces and other tribes was not formalised. In subsequent years, following the death of the Father of the Afghan Nation, as Durrani was called, it was clear that Kabul could only rule through consensus and its authority over the rest of the country would vary vastly from time to time.

Some historians are of the view that political and social dynamics in Kabul have always been out of sync with the processes at the provincial and rural levels. The rural Afghans have traditionally gone their own way, isolated in their far-flung villages and remote, difficult-to-access settlements. Over the centuries, the tribes of Afghanistan, starting with the Pashtuns, have devised their own way of resolving conflict, adjudicating disputes, and making collective decisions. The best known among these traditional mechanisms is the *jirga*, meaning assembly, usually of elders. One contemporary Afghan scholar has defined the *jirga* as a "traditional institution and gathering of the Afghans, which over the centuries, has resolved our nation's all tribal and national political, social, economic, cultural and even religious conflicts by making authoritative decisions."[2]

> The prototype in Afghanistan, the *jirga*, is the product of Pashtun tribal society and operates according to the dictates of the pashtunwali, an inclusive code of conduct guiding all aspects of Pashtun behaviour and often superseding the dictates of both Islam and the central government. Thus, in the tribal Pashtun areas, local *jirga* settles (nearly) all issues, unless assistance is requested from another tribe or the government.[3]

While the *jirga* was essentially Pashtun, something very much like it, called the *shura* was adopted by non-Pashtuns as well. The *jirgas* and *shuras* were non-state mechanisms for resolution of public conflicts. Private conflicts were usually resolved within the extended family—called *kahol* by the Pashtuns, and *kahanadan* by the Tajiks and Hazaras. These were highly formalised and ritualised mechanisms that dealt with issues at the village and higher levels.

Wardak elucidates that a *jirga* or *maraka,* as it is sometimes referred to, is not just a gathering but rather

> may be described as a local institution of dispute settlement that incorporates a prevalent (time and space-bound) *narkh*, institutionalised rituals, and a body of marakachian whose *prikra* about a dispute (or problem) is binding on the parties involved. This description indicates that *narkh*, institutionalized rituals, *marakachian* and *prikra* constitute the fundamental elements of *maraka*. Thus, an assembly of a *khel's* members without the materialisation of one, or more of these elements may be considered as an ordinary gathering rather than as a *maraka*.[4]

---

2. Rafi, H. (2002). *Loya Jirga*. Peshawar: Aman.
3. Carter, L. and K. Connor (1989). *A Preliminary Investigation of Contemporary Afghan Councils*. Peshawar: ACBAR.
4. Wardak, Ali (2003). *Jirga—A Traditional Mechanism of Conflict Resolution in Afghanistan*. UK: University of Glamorgan.

Decision-making was far from arbitrary and was based on centuries-old unwritten law called *narkh*. A Pashto saying declares: "You might abandon your tribe and homeland but you can never abandon *Narkh*." Apart from the local-level *jirgas*, there were two higher-level institutions, the *qawmi jirga* (at the level of the tribe) and *loya jirga* (at the national level).

> For centuries, Afghanistan has convened *loya jirgas*, and therefore, the whole terminology is deeply rooted in Afghan culture and history. The best known *loya jirga* in Afghan history is the one held in 1747 in Kandahar during which various Afghan tribes selected Ahmed Shah Durrani (Ahmad Shah Baba) as the first king of modern Afghanistan; he then laid down the foundation of the modern Afghan state. Also, the 1964 and 1976 *loya jirgas* have special place in Afghan modern history as women representatives, for the first time, participated in them.[5]

The Afghan jihad of the 1980s and the subsequent mujahideen wars dealt the first blows to the traditional system of conflict management. This was chiefly because the new set of commanders financed by Pakistan, the United States, and other powers were usually not local community leaders or chieftains but either outsiders or upstarts fattened with jihad money.

> Foreign military and financial aid bestowed selected militant factions with unprecedented quantity and quality of military resources. The militant factions thus gained independence from their communities and disproportionate power to deliver violence. The leaders of these selected factions, consequently, were able to corrupt the traditional ruling councils with exorbitant payments. Their incomparable military power challenged the traditional authorities in delivering justice and managing violence in accordance to customary laws.

The US-led Invasion and the Bonn Accord

On 7 October 2001, the US invaded Afghanistan with a view to destroying the Taliban, al-Qaida, and other Islamist extremists. Aided by the Afghan Northern Alliance, the US forces rapidly took over the entire country. The Taliban swiftly disappeared, mostly into neighbouring Pakistan. In December 2001, a number of hand-picked but eminent Afghans met under UN auspices in Bonn to decide on a plan for governing the country. The result was the Afghan Interim Authority (AIA) headed by Washington's choice, Hamid Karzai. The plan was sound and the aim was laudable. A government system

5. Ibid.

responsive to the needs of the people was imperative. For only such government and democratic institutions could assure that the Taliban never returned. If a progressive, modern, democratic state structure could be implanted on the anarchy that was Afghanistan, then half the problem of political Islam and terrorism could be solved. Or so were the presumptions.

Under the main terms of the Bonn Agreement, an Emergency *Loya Jirga*, chaired by the former King Zahir Shah, was to be convened within six months of the establishment of the interim authority to decide on a transitional administration to lead Afghanistan until a fully representative government could be elected, no later than two years from the date of the Emergency *Loya Jirga*. Accordingly, in June 2002, an Emergency *Loya Jirga* established a transitional administration to govern until elections could be held in 2004. According to a UK government factsheet,

> The arrangements for the *Loya Jirga* were designed to enable a broad-based representation. Seats were reserved for women, refugees, displaced persons, nomads, businessmen, intellectuals and religious scholars. The *Loya Jirga* concluded on 19 June 2002 with the inauguration of Hamid Karzai as President of the Transitional State of Afghanistan. The Emergency *Loya Jirga* marked the first opportunity for decades for the Afghan people to play a decisive role in choosing their future.

Then in January 2004, another *loya jirga* was organised and an interim constitution was agreed upon, which included the mechanism for presidential and parliamentary polls. The *jirga* approved a 162-article constitution, establishing a presidential system of government with a bicameral legislature—the *Wolesi* and the *Meshrano jirgas*. The president, both chief of state and head of government, was to be directly elected to a maximum of two five-year terms. Ministers would be nominated by the President and confirmed by the legislature. Later that year, the country held its first presidential elections where Karzai once again emerged as the winner. In September 2005, parliamentary elections were held and the country seemed set on a democratic course.

The UNDP Country Programme for the Islamic Republic of Afghanistan (2006–2008) noted:

> Since 2002, Afghanistan has made rapid political progress. *Loya Jirgas* have been convened, a constitution adopted, and elections held. The expansion of political and civil freedoms has been impressive, particularly when the conflict and repression of the previous decades are taken into consideration.

The report went on to add:

> The first objective is to strengthen the democratic state and government institutions at all levels to govern and ensure quality public services through advocacy, policy advice and capacity development. UNDP's assistance includes support to civil service reform, budget-making processes, ICT development, information management within ministries and the fight against corruption. Having paid the salaries of the police for more than two years, future support for the rule of law will include institutional development for the police...The next phase of Afghanistan's evolution requires a deepening of democracy. An accountable legislature, an independent judiciary, an active civil society and free press are necessary to secure constitutional rights for all. In this connection, access to justice is the key. Unless people have an accessible and reliable process to resolve grievances, the seeds of conflict will remain.

Unfortunately, the next phase is yet to begin. The most devastating indictment of the current political dispensation in Kabul was made by a courageous Afghan woman legislator who was expelled from parliament because in an interview she described the legislative body as worse than a stable. Twenty-nine-year-old Malalai Joya went to New York and accused the United States of making a mockery of democracy and the war on terrorism by supporting corrupt Afghan lawmakers who are criminals and warlords. "Washington supports the same enemies, who are mentally like the Taliban....They brought them back into power", soft-spoken Joya told Reuters in an interview during a visit to the United States. "Afghanistan has been fractured by rival warlords since the Soviet Union pulled out in 1989 and its Lower House of parliament, elected in 2005, is full of ex-warlords and former militia leaders along with suspected drug dealers." She recounted the horrors she experienced in parliament: "Many, many times they insulted me, even inside of the parliament they threw water at me and they threatened me with death, and one of them shouted, 'Take her and rape her'. They turned off my microphone. This is a completely non-democratic parliament, they stand up against the constitution and they do non-democratic acts." One such act was a proposal in the Lower House for a blanket amnesty for those who committed war crimes over nearly 30 years of conflict. She asked, how can criminals forgive themselves? "The Afghan people had been hopeful the US-led invasion would bring democracy for them and security for them and many more things like that, but unfortunately we are looking at a worse situation than the Taliban period."[6]

6. Reuters, 18 June 2007.

Obstacles to Institution Building

Critics of the current Afghan administration and its Western patrons believe that state institutions have not been developed because the powers that be do not wish to relinquish their control over the country. The charitable view is that the task is easier formulated than done. They argue that the restoration of law and order in the provinces has to precede developmental work, the establishment of democratic political institutions, and the gradual easing of ethnic tensions. Aid agencies either are unable to function or are functioning in less than optimal manner. Most developmental projects are way behind schedule and all this has had a negative impact on Afghan public opinion. The problem, many claim, is the failure of the military to create the necessary conditions for the implementation of administrative, developmental, and other processes. This, however, is not entirely true for both institution building and military activities at times need to go hand in hand. To be fair, there are many dilemmas in the current Afghan situation and we can discuss only a couple.

Lack of Political Will

While in theory the constitution adopted by the last *loya jirga* envisaged a democratic Afghanistan with a multilayered political decision-making and conflict resolution structure, in practice what is in place is only a top-heavy administration where all power emanates from Kabul. In Afghanistan, as in most Asian countries, there are four distinct levels of administration: the village, the district, the province, and finally the country. For the proper functioning of democracy, institutions are required at every level of the national pyramid.

In Afghanistan, as in many developing nations, the basic impediments to democracy and national-level interactions are often physical. Lack of communication, poor transportation, and telecom infrastructure has added to the rural disconnect. Millions of Afghans simply cannot participate in the democratic process or any other national process because of the physical impediments.

> Afghanistan is administratively divided into 34 provinces, near 364 districts and around 20 to 40 thousand villages. The number of districts and villages are still disputed because of the politics of power and ethnicity in the country. On the other hand there has never been a very clear definition of a village either by size of land or by population. Villages range from 25 families to 5000 families.

> On top of all, villages have continuously been disconnected with the district centres because of the accessibility problems. The average distance between a district centre and a village in Afghanistan is from one to two days walk.[7]

In the 2005 polls rural participation was negligible. According to a year 2007 estimate the Afghan population is 31.8 million. Yet, according to the official Joint Electoral Management Body (JEMB), which oversaw the polls, just about 6.4 million Afghans voted. What percentage of these votes were fake or stuffed ballots is impossible to conjecture, but it must be noted that the polls were conducted in a basically insecure environment where warlords and armed local commanders openly played a significant role. The JEMB report noted:

> Although the turnout (51.5 per cent of the total number of registration card issued) was lower than it was for last year's presidential election, the JEMB feels that it was satisfactory. Turnout was higher this year in seven provinces (including Nuristan, where the turnout nearly doubled) and among the Kuchi population, which is likely due to the higher number and better geographic spread of polling stations—across Afghanistan, there were around 30 per cent more polling stations established this year than for last year's elections. The turnout was lower in all major urban areas throughout the country, including Kabul, and throughout the Southern region. A number of factors could have contributed to this, including the requirement this year that voters only vote in the province identified on their registration cards, the large number of candidates standing for office, widespread reports of voter intimidation by candidates and their agents and persisting security issues.[8]

The 2005 polls could not, however, be described as fraudulent. The majority of Afghans who participated were extremely enthusiastic about the whole process and clearly looked forward to something positive emerging out of the entire exercise.

There is evidence of some subterfuge in the process of democratisation. In September 2005, when the parliamentary polls took place so did polls to the 34 provincial councils of the country. The provincial council elections were crucial because the upper house (*Meshrano jirga*) required the election of two candidates from each of the country's 34 provincial councils. The rest were to be filled up by Presidential nominations and by district councils that have yet to be created. So members of the provincial council were duly elected by the people in September 2005 but as of now they have little to do and no defined role whatsoever.

---

7. Rahmani, Ahmad Idrees (2005). "The Role of Religious Institutions in Local Governance and Provision of Social Service in Afghanistan", Muslim Society Group, International Policy Fellowship, September.

8. Joint Electoral Management Body (2005). *Final Report: National Assembly and Provincial Council Elections 2005*. December.

While the functions of the 249 members of the national People's Council are enumerated to a large degree in the country's constitution, the functions of the provincial councils remain largely unclear. Until the duties and authorities of those provincial bodies are more firmly enumerated and their members given official space in which to operate, there is a risk that a potentially effective mechanism for local government might be forever marginalised—and an opportunity lost.[9]

In other words, elected provincial councils do not exist.

The polity today is characterised by a multiplicity of actors. At the highest level is the presidency ensconced in Kabul, guarded by American security guards. Below that is a council of ministers. The provinces are ruled by governors appointed by Karzai. Many of them are former warlords, who remain a prominent part of the state structure because there is currently no alternative to them. Besides, the overstretched US and NATO forces have been bribing warlords to guard certain areas and fight the Taliban. Apart from this, there are no recognised offices or institutions. There are a whole lot of informal power centres, including rich NGOs, NATO and US military commanders, local Afghan commanders, ex-warlords, ISI operatives and Taliban commanders, who keep moving in and out of the country. What there is not is a working, institutionalised democracy. The average Afghan cannot be blamed for being confused and disillusioned.

Bilhol Lohdi, a somewhat mysterious but extremely cogent critic of the Karzai administration has been lambasting the current regime on several Internet sites. In one recent article he writes:

> The shibboleth that "Afghanistan is a democracy" with "a constitution, an elected president, and an elected parliament" must be consigned to the dustbin of bad jokes. The Afghan people certainly don't believe it, nor do those foreign professionals whose careers have not depended on inventing and perpetuating the myth. The claim, often forwarded by the supporters of the current Kabul setup, that there's no alternative to replace Karzai is nonsense. It is an artifice through which they hope to bamboozle the rest of the international community to help continue maintaining Karzai and their associated assets in place, despite the fact that these people are part of the problem as well as a bar to implementing a solution.

Strong words indeed!

9. Tarzi, Amin (2005). "Afghanistan: What Will Become of the Provincial Councils?", *Radio Free Europe*, 11 November.

The Ethnic Divide

A bigger and more intractable problem is the vast ethnic chasm in the country. Afghanistan has 55 ethnic groups who speak 45 languages. However, the Pashtuns have traditionally ruled Afghanistan and believe that they alone are destined to rule the country. They reject the notion of power sharing with the other ethnic groups like the Hazaras, Tajiks, and Uzbeks. As one scholar has pointed out, Pashtuns call people speaking Dari (a Persian dialect) Tajiks.

> The Tajiks themselves, however, never use that ethnonym, preferring to use the name of the valleys they come from to identify themselves, such as Panjshiri, Munjani and Andarabi. They identify with a place, not a tribe, nor its mythical origins, like the Pashtuns do. By using the spatial ethnonym "Tajik," the Pashtuns are, in a sense, denying Tajiks a territorial basis in Afghanistan and therefore are discrediting their right to spatial representation in any government in Kabul.[10]

Since 1880, when the British created the state of Afghanistan, there have been massive internal population movements at the instigation of the Pashtun royalty as part of their plan to Pashtunise the country. Even though King Zahir Shah, the Pashtun royal ruler, was ousted in 1973, the quest to Pashtunise the country did not end. In fact, it continued with the Taliban government, which seized power in 1996. Taliban comes from a Pashto suffix attached to the Arabic word "talib". The Taliban were both an ethnic movement and a religious one. Twenty-six out of twenty-seven members of the Taliban government's leadership were Pashtun and they were determined to bring the various ethnic groups of Afghanistan under traditional Pashtun conservative rural culture.

> The carnage wrought by the Pashtun Taliban in the Kuh Daman valley, the orchards and breadbasket that sustained the Kabul area for millennia, were pulverised by the Taliban in 1999. The Taliban used a scorched-earth policy to destroy the Kohestani ("Tajik") *manteqas*, for they knew each *manteqa* had a commander who could marshal support from his collateral neighbours to oppose them.[11]

Karzai's cabinet initially had a preponderance of leaders belonging to the erstwhile Northern Alliance, which had supported and fought for the US-led alliance. The Northern Alliance leaders were dependable and united in their hatred of the Taliban. Thus, the three most powerful men in President Karzai's first cabinet were Tajik leaders:

---

10. Allan, Nigel J.R. (2003). "Rethinking Governance in Afghanistan", *Journal of International Affairs*, Spring.

11. Ibid.

Marshall Mohammad Fahim, leader of the Northern Alliance, Defence Minister; Abdullah Abdullah, another Northern Alliance strongman, Foreign Minister; and Yunus Qanooni, the political and military heir of Ahmad Shah Masood, Interior Minister. They were the best known faces of the new Afghan government after Hamid Karzai.

The Pashtun population, in general, was mortified and felt that the Tajiks had taken over their country. Karzai consequently has been steadily trying to weed out the prominent Northern Alliance warlords from his cabinet. Qanooni was the first to go because he was unwise enough to challenge Karzai's leadership. He was first demoted to education minister. He then challenged Karzai in the presidential elections and came second, but found himself without a job. He is currently the speaker of the *Wolesi jirga*. Qanooni floated a new political alliance in March 2005 named Jabahai Tafahim Millie (National Understanding Front), declaring that his aim was to try to change the strong presidential system into a parliamentary system.

In end-December 2004, in a cabinet reshuffle Karzai sacked Marshal Mohammad Fahim as defence minister and replaced him by his deputy Abdul Rahim Wardak, a Pashtun. Karzai named a relatively unknown Habibullah Qaderi to head the new Counter-Narcotics Ministry, which will be tasked with cracking down on a multibillion-dollar drug trade that is flooding the world with cheap heroin. Southern warlord Gul Agha Sherzai has been removed as public works minister. Also dropped from the cabinet was Sayed Hussain Anwari, who controlled a private army in the north and had been agriculture minister. The well-known warlord and governor of Herat, Ismail Khan, was given a minor position in the cabinet.

On 22 March 2006 in another reshuffle, fourteen ministers were retained, eight new ones were appointed, and three were reshuffled. Abdullah Abdullah, a Tajik and a key figure was dropped as foreign minister and replaced by Dr. Rangeen Dadfar Spanta, a Karzai confidant. This reshuffle ended the dominance of the Northern Alliance triumvirate in Karzai's government. The Pashtuns, however, are far from satisfied. Of the 28 ministers (including temporary ministers) currently in the cabinet, 10 are Pashtun, 9 Tajiks, 5 Hazara, 2 Uzbek, 1 Baloch, and 1 Turkmen.

A number of experts are sceptical about the prospects of success of the current political system imposed on Afghans by the Bonn Accord. "The building of an Afghan nation with strong central control, put forth in 2001 in Bonn and the 2002 follow-up meeting, is a fantasy of social democratic European governments." The solution for Afghanistan may instead lie in considering and implementing the features of a co-imperium form of governance. According to Alain Coret's definition,

> a coimperium is a regime in which a partial international community exercises certain competencies over a portion of the territory of a third state...All regions of the country must be able to participate in decisions that affect them. This involves maintaining indigenous suzerainty by creating regions dominated by particular ethnic groups that have a powerful presence both at the local and national levels.[12]

There does not appear to be any urgency on the part of the powers behind Karzai to radically alter the present political order, wherein Kabul controls all institutions and political processes in the country. There is a legitimate fear of things going out of hand and Karzai's weak hold on the rest of the country becoming untenable. The focus clearly is on the fight against the Taliban which, instead of diminishing over the years, has only exacerbated since last year.

Alternative Models

Max Weber postulated the existence of three forms of authority: traditional, rational-legal, and charismatic. Charismatic authority, according to Weber, is a kind of exceptional (or divine) endowment of grace that is imputed by followers to leaders. Contemporary examples of this form of authority may be the authority of Mahatma Gandhi or Nelson Mandela. Legal-rational authority, on the other hand, is the authority of highly organised groups such as that of the modern state. And finally traditional authority for Weber is the semi-political decisions made by chiefs of tribes in societies where formal processes of governance do not exist or are not fully institutionalised.

In the absence of a charismatic leader in Afghanistan, perhaps, one solution for Afghanistan could be hybridisation of Weber's traditional and rational-legal models. The *jirga* model is a rather sophisticated and

12. Ibid.

accepted form of institution, which could be formalised, enmeshed with the state structure, and legitimised. The precise form of such hybrid politico-judicial-executive institutions would emerge through experimentation, given the necessary political will. After all, the acceptability of the *jirga* concept was successfully used to confer legitimacy to the post–Bonn Accord institutions and to the current Afghan constitution. If the *jirga* could work at the highest level, there is no reason why it cannot work at the lower levels of Afghan society where conflict resolution institutions are needed the most.

Unfortunately, instead of seeking viable solutions to the pressing problem of institution building, Afghanistan of late has been subject to several bizarre experiments. One is the outsourcing of governance to NGOs, a prominent example of which is the National Solidarity Programme (NSP). The NSP was one of the original 12 National Priority Programmes (NPP) of the government and was first announced in President Karzai's address to donors at the Tokyo Conference in January 2007. The aim was to establish stable state structures for development. But nothing seems to have come of this. Like most other local bodies, the local development councils too appear to be dominated or under the influence of former religious leaders, *Arbabs* or local strongmen. Thus, traditional society leaders and the common Afghan have been rendered irrelevant to the political decision-making process. Despite the change of regime, very little has changed at the grassroots.

Ironically, the epilogue to the series of unfortunate events in Afghanistan is best provided by President Karzai, who, during a visit to the United States, lamented: "All politicians in this system have acquired everything—money, lots of money. God knows it is beyond the limit. The banks of the world are full of the money of our statesmen. The luxurious houses [built in Afghanistan in the past five years] belong to members of the government and parliament, not only in Kabul but here and there. Every one of them have three or four houses in different countries...With the support of the world community—money, aircraft, and their soldiers—and with full sympathy of the Afghan people, the Afghan politicians were able to return to their country. Unfortunately, I see now that they did not learn the lessons of the past. They should know that the Afghan people will rise against us. And this time, there will be no place [abroad] for us to flee."

But who, pray, allowed all that to happen?

Afghanistan Timeline

2001

7 October: The US, Britain launch air strikes against Afghanistan after the Taliban refuse to hand over Osama bin Laden, held responsible for the 11 September 2001 attacks on America.

12 November: Alliance march into abandoned Kabul and other key cities.

5 December: Afghan groups agree to deal in Bonn for interim government.

7 December: The Taliban give up their last stronghold of Kandahar, but Mullah Omar remains at large.

22 December: Pashtun royalist, Hamid Karzai is sworn in as head of a 30-member interim power-sharing government.

2002

January: First contingent of foreign peacekeepers in place.

17 April: Former king Zahir Shah returns, but says he makes no claim to the throne.

13 June: *Loya Jirga*, or grand council, elects Hamid Karzai as interim head of state. Karzai picks members of his administration which is to serve until 2004.

2003

11 August: NATO takes control of security in Kabul, its first-ever operational commitment outside Europe.

2004

4 January: Grand Assembly (*Loya Jirga*) adopts new constitution, which provides for strong presidency.

9 October: Presidential elections.

3 November: Hamid Karzai is declared the winner in the Presidential elections, with 55 per cent of the vote. He is sworn in, amid tight security, in December.

2005

18 September: First parliamentary and provincial elections in more than 30 years.

December: New parliament holds its inaugural session.

2006

July onwards: NATO troops takeover the leadership of military operations in the south. Fierce fighting ensues as the forces try to extend government control in areas where the Taliban influence is strong.

October: NATO assumes responsibility for security across the whole of Afghanistan, taking command in the east from US-led coalition force.

2007

22 July: Former king Zahir Shah dies.

10

Civil-Military Engagement in Post-Conflict Reconstruction

A Study of Provincial Reconstruction Teams in Afghanistan

SEEMA SRIDHAR

The US war on terror that began with Operation Enduring Freedom (OEF) in October 2001 has set in motion the arduous long-drawn task of post-conflict reconstruction in Afghanistan. The manifold responsibilities that the US and its allies have taken upon themselves include setting up a capable Afghan security force; strengthening NATO presence; improving provincial governance and developing Afghanistan's rural economy; tackling the problem of poppy cultivation; fighting corruption; and reforming the judicial system. The end of war does not necessarily entail restoration of security. The initiation of a cease-fire, peace agreement or even efforts at disarmament of warring parties do not necessarily assure improvements in the safety of either civilians or former combatants. In fact, many so-called post-conflict environments pose even more direct and indirect threats to civilians than the armed conflicts that preceded them. The post-conflict designation disguises a vast array of real and perceived threats facing most societies emerging from war.[1] Peace, development, and democracy are three interwoven dimensions in such a scenario. They are mutually reinforcing. Democracy is a precursor. To ensure that disparities are not too wide, creating the potential for rebellion and violence, equitable distribution of economic progress, and sustainable development is necessary.

1. Muggah, Robert (2005). "No Magic Bullet: A Critical Perspective on Disarmament, Demobilization and Reintegration (DDR) and Weapons Reduction in Post-conflict Contexts", *Round Table* 94(379): 239–52 (April).

Evolving international regulatory mechanisms aimed at addressing cases of state "collapse" or at shoring up "failing states" is one of the pressing questions in US foreign policy agenda. The 2002 US National Security Strategy Report states: "America is now threatened less by conquering states than we are by failing ones."[2] In August 2004, the US government established a state-building department, the Office of the Coordinator for Reconstruction and Stabilisation. In September 2005, the UN world summit followed suit and agreed on the establishment of a proposed Peace-Building Commission to coordinate international activity in this area.[3]

Following the ouster of the Taliban regime, the starting point for rebuilding Afghanistan was the "Agreement on Provisional Arrangements in Afghanistan Pending Re-establishment of Permanent Institutions"—the Bonn Agreement—signed by the representatives of various Afghan tribes and groups on 5 December 2001. The agreement established an Interim Afghan Authority, with the 1964 Afghan constitution as its foundation. It also laid down a timetable for establishing a new government, framing a new constitution, and ultimately elections. In comparison to the successful US military campaign, the political task of creating a stable and secure democratic state in Afghanistan is proving much more difficult. The Afghan government continues to be severely hampered in addressing people's grievances. The absence of adequate funds, underdeveloped security structures, and economic infrastructure are formidable roadblocks. The most compelling challenges facing Afghanistan today are: setting up a broad-based central government, managing centre-periphery relations, especially in dealing with warlords; providing credible security to people and extending the rule of law beyond Kabul; quickening the pace of economic reconstruction; maintaining ethnic harmony, and above all, achieving national integration.

---

2. The National Security Strategy of the United States of America, The White House Website, at <*http://www.whitehouse.gov/nsc/nss.html*>
3. United Nations General Assembly Resolution, A/RES/60/180, 30 December 2005, at <*http://daccessdds.un.org/doc/UNDOC/GEN/N05/498/40/PDF/N0549840.pdf*>

Peace Support Operations—Key Concepts

According to the British Army Manual on Peace Support Operations, "PSOs are multifunctional operations in which impartial military activities are designed to create a secure environment and to facilitate the efforts of the civilian elements of the mission to create a self-sustaining peace."[4] PSOs may include peacekeeping and peace enforcement, conflict prevention, peacemaking, peace-building, and humanitarian operations.[5] Peace Support Force (PSF) is a military force assigned to a peace support operation.

Peacemaking is a PSO, conducted after the initiation of a conflict to secure a ceasefire or peaceful settlement that involves primarily diplomatic action supported, when necessary, by direct or indirect use of military assets.[6] Peace enforcement is a PSO conducted to maintain a ceasefire or a peace agreement where the level of consent and compliance is uncertain, and the threat of disruption is high. Peacekeeping is a PSO following an agreement or ceasefire that has established a permissive environment where the level of consent and compliance is high, and the threat of disruption is low. The use of force by peacekeepers is usually limited to self-defence. *Peace-building* is a PSO employing complementary diplomatic, civil and, when necessary, military means, to address the underlying causes of conflict and the longer-term needs of the people. It requires a commitment to a long-term process and may run concurrently with other types of PSOs.[7] The PRT (provincial reconstruction team) concept does not fit into any of these heads, but comprises traces of characteristics of all of these operations.

Access to local populations is crucial for reconstruction and state-building activities. This access depends on the acceptance of the PSF by the local populations. Civil-military engagement and the direct involvement of military forces in humanitarian assistance are means of gaining local consent. It was a strategy to "win hearts and minds"

4. British Army, Design for military operations, British Military Doctrine, 1996.
5. "Peace Support Operations Manual, A Working Draft for African Military Practitioners", 2000 February, at <*http://www.iss.co.za/Pubs/Other/PeaceSupportManualMM/Contents.html*>; also, <*http://www.trainingforpeace.org/themes/supp.htm*>
6. Ibid.
7. Ibid.

in the context of OEF. The strategy was a response to mounting antipathy toward the coalition among the majority Pashtun community in the south and east of the country, where the bulk of military operations have been undertaken, and to international criticism of the obvious divide between OEF, and the wider reconstruction and stabilisation process.

PRTs: Structure and Function

The PRTs were undertaken as an experiment in civil-military engagement in Afghanistan. These are military-run enclaves designed to provide havens for international aid workers. A PRT, composed of 80 to 100 inter-agency personnel from a number of countries including Afghanistan, is in charge of wide-ranging activities, from resolving local disputes to coordinating local reconstruction projects, although the US-run PRTs focus mostly on counter-insurgency. They attempt to address the security needs of Afghans through a comprehensive approach involving military, development, and political personnel.

The diversity in the range of tasks for potential UN engagement in the pursuit of peace and security was first laid out in Boutros Boutros-Ghali's "An Agenda for Peace". They are listed as preventative diplomacy, peacemaking, peacekeeping, and the "critically related concept of post-conflict peace-building."[8]

The PRTs were established in Afghanistan in order to enable the international community to provide improved security, extend the writ of the central government into the hinterlands, and facilitate reconstruction and economic development throughout the country. They intended to monitor conditions and the progress of ongoing reconstruction efforts. PRTs coordinate with the NGOs for reasons of flexibility and efficiency. To facilitate cooperation, initial PRT locations were deliberately chosen to be co-located with the existing United Nations Office for the Coordination of Humanitarian Affairs (UNOCHA) regional offices.[9]

---

8. Boutros-Ghali, Boutros (1992). "An Agenda for Peace: Preventive diplomacy, peacemaking and peace-keeping", A/47/277-S/24111, Report of the Secretary-General pursuant to the statement adopted by the Summit Meeting of the Security Council on 31 January, at <*http://www.un.org/Docs/SG/agpeace.html*>

9. United Nations Office for the Coordination of Humanitarian Affairs (UNOCHA), at <*http://www.ochaopt.org/*>

Prior to the establishment of the first PRTs, Coalition Humanitarian Liaison Cells (CHLCs) and US Army Civil Affairs Teams–Afghanistan (CAT-As) supported humanitarian assistance, relief, and reconstruction efforts throughout Afghanistan. Civilian reconstruction activities were constrained by the lack of an international security presence in outlying provinces. OEF was focused on combat operations, and the International Security Assistance Force (ISAF) was restricted to Kabul and its environs with little likelihood of near-term expansion.

In April 2002, President Bush referred to the success of George C. Marshall's vision to rebuild Europe and Japan after World War II, and suggested a "Marshall Plan for Afghanistan."[10] The Department of Defence (DoD), the Department of State, and the US Agency for International Development (USAID) developed a concept to employ interagency civil-military field teams throughout Afghanistan. The US Central Command (CENTCOM, headquartered in Tampa, Florida) whose area of responsibility stretches from the Horn of Africa to Central Asia, devised a plan to implement this concept using Joint Regional Teams (JRTs). From the outset in December 2002, Hamid Karzai, the interim president of the Afghan Transitional Authority, was an enthusiastic supporter of the concept. At his request, the name was changed from JRTs to provincial reconstruction teams to indicate the purpose as providing support to the government (as opposed to regional power brokers or "warlords"), and to denote reconstruction as the principal activity of the teams.

The PRTs engage key government, military, tribal, village, and religious leaders in the provinces, while monitoring and reporting on important political, military, and reconstruction developments. They work with Afghan authorities to provide security, including support for key events such as the constitutional *Loya Jirga*, presidential and parliamentary elections, and the disarmament, demobilisation and reintegration of militia forces. They assist in the deployment and mentoring of Afghan National Army and police units assigned to the provinces. In partnership with the Afghan government, the UN, other donors and NGOs, PRTs provide needed development and

10. "President Outlines War Effort", Remarks by the President to the George C. Marshall ROTC Award Seminar on National Security, Cameron Hall, Virginia Military Institute, Lexington, Virginia, 4 April 2002, at <*http://www.whitehouse.gov/news/releases/2002/04/20020417-1.html*>

humanitarian assistance. In some cases, they directly support assistance projects that address local needs and build Afghan capacity. While the military staff consists of a mix of civil affairs officers, quick reaction forces, monitoring teams and infantry from a variety of services, the political staff is provided by the State Department in the case of the US, and the Foreign and Commonwealth Office (FCO) in the case of the UK. Development expertise is provided by USAID and DFID for the US and UK PRTs respectively. The PRT's military component is intended to include the following staff—Commanding Officer and his immediate staff; Army Civil Affairs Teams (two teams, four soldiers on each team); Military Police Unit (three soldiers); Psychological Operations Unit; Explosive Ordnance/De-mining Unit; Intelligence Team; Medics; Force Protection Unit (infantry platoon of forty soldiers); Administrative and support personnel.[11] Most PRTs are, however, understaffed by this criterion.

The first US PRT was established in Gardez in December 2002.[12] There are currently 25 PRTs. Twelve are US-led (Asadabad, Bagram/Parwan, Farah, Gardez, Ghazni, Jalalabad, Kala Gush, Khost, Mehtarlam, Panjshir, Qalat and Sharana), primarily in eastern Afghanistan; the rest are led by New Zealand (Bamian), Lithuania (Chaghcharan), Germany (Feyzabad and Kunduz), Italy (Herat), Canada (Kandahar), UK (Lashkar Gah), Norway (Maimana), Sweden (Mazar-e Sharif), Hungary (Pol-e Khumri), Spain (Qal-e Now), the Netherlands (Tarin Kowt), and Turkey (Wardak).[13]

Criticisms

Co-ordination. From the perspective of NGHAs (non-governmental humanitarian agencies),[14] the relationship was destined to be highly

11. Perito, Robert M. (2005). "The U.S. Experience with Provincial Reconstruction Teams in Afghanistan: Lessons Identified", USIP Special Report 152. October, at <*www.usip.org/specialists/bios/current/perito.html*>

12. USAID, "A Snapshot of Provincial Reconstruction Teams", at <*www.usaid.gov/locations/asia_near_east/countries/afghanistan/prt.html*>

13. Dziedzic, Michael J. and Colonel Michael K. Seidl (2005). "Provincial Reconstruction Teams and Military Relations with International and Nongovernmental Organizations in Afghanistan", USIP Special Report 147. September, at <*http://www.usip.org/pubs/specialreports/sr147.pdf*>

14. The term "non-governmental humanitarian agencies" (NGHAs) encompasses national and international humanitarian non-governmental organisations (NGOs); the International Committee of the Red Cross (ICRC); and the humanitarian agencies within the UN system.

problematic given the PRTs' inextricable links to the coalition rather than to a UN-mandated peacekeeping force. NGO criticism has continued to focus on the failure of the coalition clearly to define PRTs' mandate or terms of reference or to address the security situation and its choice of focus, i.e., assistance type activities. No overarching framework or strategic guidelines have been established for PRT deployments, and the wider debate on the subject remains highly polarised. PRTs led and staffed by various governments in the coalition are considerably influenced by their respective governments in day-to-day operations. Thus, there are hitches in coordination and the implementation of a united effort throughout Afghanistan is rendered difficult. As more PRTs transition to NATO/ISAF control and more nations assume responsibility, the challenges associated with coordination and harmonisation of functions could increase.

Consent, Impartiality and Use of Force. Consent, the first tenet of the trinity principles in any peacekeeping operation, in the case of PRTs is inconsistent and shallow. The practice of supporting warlords and their armies for short-term gains by incorporating them in the electoral process deciphers into a form of consent by co-option. So long as the promise of material or political gains are still on offer, regional warlords would allow continued PRTs access to populations as long as they benefit with political incentives that cloak them with legitimacy. But once there is a rupture in this mutually beneficial relationship, warlords will have little to gain from cooperation with the PRTs. This could lead to direct combat. Moreover, associating with the powerful warlords by the PRTs result in disillusionment among the common people, who suffer because of the atrocities of these warlords. The needs assessment programme carried out by the PRTs also tends to be superficial as the method adopted is in the form of brief consultation with the local chieftain regarding the facilities lacking in the respective areas. The needs of women, minorities, former combatants, and other groups that need special care in a volatile post-conflict situation are not addressed. The purpose of bringing stability in the long run therefore, is not served through this mechanism. And of course, the principle of consent is not upheld in the true spirit of the term.

According to Meinrad Studer of the International Committee for the Red Cross (ICRC), the ICRC "saw from the start the danger of humanitarian efforts becoming integrated into a political process and thereby themselves becoming politicised."[15] Studer identifies several disadvantages of militaries delivering humanitarian assistance. First, humanitarian action carried out by military forces will invariably be compromised as soon as their mission requires them to use force. Second, militaries will often succumb to the temptation to instrumentalise humanitarian assistance in order to secure the compliance of warring parties or to gather intelligence. Third, the delivery of humanitarian assistance may divert the military from its *raison d'être,* the maintenance and enforcement of security. Finally, the conflation of humanitarian and military mandates "risks turning humanitarian workers into perceived enemy agents and thus jeopardising their personal safety."[16] These points have been reiterated by NGHAs and analysts over the last few years. This rift was brought to the forefront in the summer of 2004, when Médicins Sans Frontieres (MSF), which had worked in the country for over 24 years, suspended its operations in Afghanistan after the shooting deaths of five of its employees by anti-government militants in June 2004.[17] MSF attributed its decision to the proliferation of the PRTs, which it argued had blurred the lines between the civilian and military spheres and placed its staff at undue risk. This concern is shared by several NGHAs which have refused to be associated with the PRTs. The use of soldiers in humanitarian aid projects makes it difficult for the locals and the hostile parties to distinguish between non-combatant aid workers and soldiers, thereby placing NGO personnel at greater risk and also creating a problem of trust while dealing with locals. Caroline Douillez, a spokesperson for the ICRC in Kabul said, "As a general position, we feel it creates confusion in the minds of those who receive the aid and creates confusion among those who carry out military and humanitarian missions at the same time."[18] Barbara J. Stapleton,

15. Studer, M. (2001). "The ICRC and Civil-Military Relations in Armed Conflict", *International Review of the Red Cross* 83(842): 372 (June), at <*http://www.jca.apc.org/~jann/Documents/Civil%20Military%20Relations.pdf*>

16. Ibid.: 374–5.

17. "MSF leaves country following staff killings and threats", MSF Activity Reports on Afghanistan December 2004, at <*http://www.doctorswithoutborders.org/news/afghanistan.cfm*>

Advocacy and Policy Coordinator, Agency Coordinating Body for Afghan Relief (ACBAR), Kabul in her report states that:

> The core concern of international NGOs was that Afghan perceptions of their impartiality and neutrality would be eroded by their direct contact with Coalition civil-military units with potentially adverse effects on future operational capacity and a belief that a PRT presence may further increase their security problems. Afghan NGO staff voiced concerns to international partners that in an uncertain future, any involvement with the Coalition-led PRTs would expose them as targets. All NGOs agreed that as PRTs were being conducted under the aegis of the Coalition, their presence and the activities they engaged in, further confused an already highly complex situation.[19]

The primary argument is that the concept of PRTs violates the fundamental humanitarian precept that aid must be provided in a neutral and impartial manner based solely on the criteria of need, i.e., aid should not be politicised. The Afghans associate PRTs with OEF. PRTs operate under the same command structure and receive air support from the coalition as and when required. Coalition combat operations still continue in the southern and south-eastern provinces of Afghanistan, and as long as this continues, the principle of neutrality of the PRTs cannot be upheld. The British Army's own golden rule of impartiality—that "the referee must not become a party to the conflict"[20]—is broken.

The argument that it does not uphold the third principle of PSOs—non-use of force—can be technically rebutted on the grounds that PRTs have a robust self-defence capability but do not have enough resources and personnel to launch operations. Even during hostilities they draw from the coalition bases stationed close to them.

Encroaching Humanitarian Space and Duplication. It is a further encroachment of "humanitarian space" traditionally occupied by the NGO community. A clear distinction between civilian and military roles is vital for the preservation of humanitarian space. Even before the inception of PRTs, coalition troops have also been involved in small-scale "humanitarian" and "reconstruction" activities. Their

---

18. Center for Humanitarian Cooperation (2003). "The Provincial Reconstruction Team (PRT) in Afghanistan and its Role in Reconstruction", 31 May, at <*http://www.reliefweb.int/w/rwb.nsf/0/7fa2a04b0431553b85256d6a00740fe2?OpenDocument*>

19. Stapleton, Barbara J. Bonn (2003). "The Provincial Reconstruction Team Plan in Afghanistan: A New Direction?" Agency Coordinating Body for Afghan Relief (ACBAR) Paper, May, at <*www.agafghanistan.de/arg/arp/stapleton.pdf*>

20. British Army (1998). *Peace Support Operations: Joint Warfare Publication 3-50*. London: HMSO.

seeming encroachment into humanitarian territory prior to the development of the PRT concept when US civil affairs officers were seen posing as humanitarian workers in Afghanistan in March 2002 invited serious condemnation from NGHAs. NGHA representatives wrote to the US Government representatives, requesting that:

> ...transparency be maintained in any military involvement in civil affairs operations. Soldiers (and intelligence officers) should in no case claim to be in Afghanistan as humanitarian workers. In addition, all military personnel involved in conducting civil affairs operations should be in uniform and clearly identifiable as soldiers at all times. The humanitarian community objects in the strongest possible terms to armed soldiers dressing in civilian clothes in order to engage in civil assistance programmes.[21]

Assistance agencies view direct PRT support for humanitarian and reconstruction projects with severe suspicion. The parent governments have been accused of overtly politicising and militarising aid. Funding is provided by the US DoD from within its Overseas Humanitarian Disaster and Civic Aid (OHDACA) budget.[22] The OHDACA guidelines require conformity of projects with emergency/humanitarian-style priorities and needs. US PRT spending has predominantly focused on drilling wells, rebuilding schools and clinics, and some road resurfacing.[23] These are often sectors where NGHAs already have substantial capacity to cover basic needs, resulting in unnecessary duplication of assistance. In the UK model of PRTs, costs for reconstruction-style projects are covered by DFID, which allows for relative flexibility as to the type of programmes selected for support.[24] In principle, DFID states that "development projects will be selected with care in consultation with local development actors so as to avoid duplication or interference with activities already being undertaken."

The major point of contention by the NGHAs that PRTs duplicate services and projects already available and provided by the international

---

21. The NGO Forum, Kabul (2002). "The Need for a Clear Distinction between Humanitarian Programme and Military Activities in Afghanistan", March, at <*http://www/euronaid.nl/archive/Soldiers*>
22. CRS Report for Congress RL32090, "FY2004 Supplemental Appropriations for Iraq, Afghanistan, and the Global War on Terrorism: Military Operations & Reconstruction Assistance", by Stephen Daggett, Larry Nowels, Curt Tarnoff, and Rhoda Margesson, 15 October 2003, at <*http://www.fas.org/man/crs/RL32090.pdf*>
23. Borders, Robert (2004). "Provincial Reconstruction Teams in Afghanistan: A Model for Post-Conflict Reconstruction and Development", *Journal of Development and Social Transformation* vol.1 (November), at <*http://www.maxwell.syr.edu/moynihan/programs/dev/pdfs/borders1.pdf*>
24. DFID Western Asia Department, Afghanistan: Provincial Reconstruction Teams Project Memorandum, June 2003, at <*http://dfidweb.dfid.gov.uk/prismdocs/ASIA_AND_PACIFIC_DIVISION/137581005p1.doc*>

aid community are somewhat assuaged by the DFID model, which adheres to the International Development Act.[25] Development projects undertaken by PRTs are viewed as public relations exercises to win the goodwill of the international community and the local Afghan population for the coalition's commitment to reconstruction and stabilisation in Afghanistan. NGHAs also claim that NGOs are a much cheaper alternative to reconstruction than bringing in the military.[26] This claim, however, has not been verified by any statistical data. An important observation in this regard by Robert Borders of the United States Army is that PRTs use local labour and they predominantly operate in areas where NGOs either will not or cannot operate because of security concerns.[27]

Another contention against PRTs is that it distracts the military from its primary mission and responsibility of providing security. PRTs have particular problems in maintaining security due to their small size, lack of combat power, and the isolated environment in which they operate. They are also a poor substitute for the ISAF in terms of the manpower, reach, and capabilities necessary to ensure the safety of NGHAs operating in the country. The level of security required by NGHAs is not within the intended charter of the reconstruction teams. That security task belongs to regular combat troops who are manned, equipped, and trained to accomplish it, similar to the NATO forces already in the country. It is not a substitute for a robust peace-support mission and lacks the capacity to launch offensive operations or to intervene in large-scale factional disputes. The presence of PRTs is designed to serve as a deterrent to insurgents and criminals who had been active in these areas. Use of close air support and quick reaction forces is available to coalition PRTs and has been utilised while confronted by hostile forces. NATO had designed a plan that calls for the creation of a combat brigade to support PRTs in each

25. International Development Act 2002, at <*http://opsi.gov.uk/acts/acts2002/ukpga_20020001_en_1*>. This Act was passed on 26 February 2002 to make provision relating to the provision of assistance for countries outside the United Kingdom; to make provision with respect to certain international financial institutions and the Commonwealth Scholarship Commission; and for connected purposes.

26. UNOCHA, Integrated Regional Information Network (IRIN) (2003). "Afghanistan: Focus on Coalition Reconstruction Teams", February, at <*http://www.irinnews.org/report.asp?ReportID=32509&SelectRegion=Central_Asia&SelectCountry=AFGHANISTAN*>

27. Borders, "Provincial Reconstruction Teams...", n.23, p.10.

designated region of the country. The mere existence of the combat brigade would serve as a "force multiplier". However, lack of resources has shelved the plan.

Questions have been raised about the capacity of the military for this type of work. The training, organisation, self-sustenance, and discipline necessary for operations that require a rapid response are found in the military set-up. Highly effective communication systems; speedy transportation of large volumes of material to emergency situations; good stocking of resources often in short supply in emergencies; medical care equipment which can also be put to use to serve local populations; emergency skills such as engineering, logistical support, mine clearance, etc., render the military suitable for providing life-saving assistance when even humanitarian agencies are denied access. In other words, military involvement is generally acceptable as a "last resort" in emergencies and as a second option to ISAF for providing security. Since the PRTs are seen to be duplicating activities rather than providing assistance that is beyond the realm of the NGHAs in the Afghan context, the rift between the two continues.

Conclusion

The PRT concept has proven to be a flexible model. Its biggest problem is the lack of a coherently defined mandate and a clear strategic framework. The PRTs need to first define who they are and what roles are primary for them, and fulfil these roles in that order of priority. Being different from traditional PSOs, they should be seen as an evolving model. Civil and military actors can continue to work together in a collaborative effort to build peace, each capitalising on their strengths, and realising the limitations of their capabilities and work accordingly. Focus on security, implementing humanitarian assistance only in complex emergency situations to complement the efforts of NGHAs, focus on infrastructure rehabilitation and security sector reform (SSR) rather then "quick impact" development projects, clearly demarcating themselves from humanitarian actors, refraining from utilising aid conditionality, more local civilian participation—these are a few steps that might further streamline the role of PRTs to make them more acceptable to other actors, and also enhance efficiency in operations.

The United States Institute for Peace (USIP) recommends that a mechanism should be created to permit a regular dialogue between NGHAs and the US government offices at the Department of State and DoD that are responsible for stabilisation and reconstruction policy. USIP and the US Army Peacekeeping and Stability Operations Institute should work with the Department of State, DoD, and the NGO community in the United States to establish a permanent mechanism for this purpose.[28] It also recommends that the Peacekeeping Best Practices Unit of the UN Department of Peacekeeping Operations should be used by the NGO community to disseminate guidelines and lessons learned to troop-contributing countries. The civil-military community needs to be engaged so that its future course of development can be shaped to make certain that all stakeholder interests and concerns are addressed. This last point is especially pertinent given the potential for applying the PRT model in Iraq as well.

28. USIP Special Report 147, "Provincial Reconstruction Teams and Military Relations...", n.13, p.13.

Index

K

L

M

N

O

P

Q

R

S

T

U

W